Musings from the Bay

Stories from Delaware Bay's Past

Musings from the Bay
James Milton Hanna

ISBN 1-930052-39-1
Library of Congress Number 2007926306

History and incidents occurring on Delaware Bay.
Stories of Watermen, Trappers and Recreational Boaters.

Library of Congress Cataloging in Publication Data
Musings from the Bay
Stories of incidents occurring on or near Delaware Bay.
Fishing, hunting, boating, crabbing, oystering and trapping.
Historical

Other books by author:

Cornbread and Beans for Breakfast
A Possum in Every pot
Beyond Yonder Ridge
Shiloh
Southern Tales
Once Upon a Time in the South
Milton's Guide to Self Publishing
Tales from Delaware Bay
More Tales from Delaware Bay
The Labrador Saga
Meandering Around Delaware Bay

Cherokee Books
24 Meadow Ridge Pkwy
Dover, DE 19904

Dedication/ Acknowledgments To:

Donna Chappell for editing.

The watermen who shared their stories.

Paul Davis for his input of the cabin story.

Captain Willis Hand and his wife.

"Big Daddy" Mills for his input.

The Interpretative Center at Port Penn

And most of all, those who still earn their livelihood from Delaware Bay.

Table of Contents

Foreword

The Delaware Bay is truly a remarkable body of water. The events and incidents occurring on the Bay are amazing. Those who work on the water and those who use the Bay for recreational purposes witness many unusual incidents that can place people in peril. Often the perilous situations occurring on the Bay are caused by ignorance. People do wrong things while on the water such as too much speed for prevailing wave conditions, improper anchoring of boats and general ignorance of boating. That's what causes many problems! There is no excuse for running out of gas on the Bay, but it still happens. And then, there are the accidents that can beset the most experienced waterman. A sudden storm or equipment breakdown is always a possibility for those who work on Delaware Bay.

Men who have worked the Bay as a vocation for years — and they are getting fewer and fewer each year — are filled with dismay about the declining catches of crabs and the limited allotment of oysters that can be harvested from the Bay. The abundance of fish that once brought thousands of sport fishermen to Delaware Bay is only a memory to many.

People who still earn a living from the murky waters of the Bay have to work smarter under existing shellfish regulations and with the shortage of marketable shellfish.

Some still earn a respectful livelihood by pursuing various aspects in harvesting the bounty of the Bay. I am sure that some of these men often ask themselves the question, "Why am I still trying to earn a living from the Bay?" Actually, none would give up their lifestyle of independence for any other type of work. Yet, they wonder what the future holds.

Whenever I'm on the water or see the many boats working back and forth on the Bay, I'm truly amazed that there aren't more fatalities on the Bay. Sometimes those who have worked on the water for many years, shake their heads in disbelief at the things they witness supposedly grown men do while boating on the Bay.

The Bay is in remarkably good condition considering three hundred years of activity. In my time, living near the water, I have seen many changes, especially erosion, silting and the decline in shellfish and fish. Yet, the Bay still calls people and the future of the Bay is still unknown. Pollution and an unbalanced supply of shellfish and fish should concern all of us who love the Bay. Preserving memories of Delaware Bay as it once was is the purpose of this book.

JMH 2007

Delaware Bay

Before the sun smiles on a new day, when only a hint in the eastern sky, motors start with puffballs of white smoke disrupting the quietness of the coming day.

Boats leave a silver wake as they glide down river harking to the broad waters that seem to call, "Come, see what I have for you this day." Guess!

Will it be feast or famine? Only I know, but you will have to seek by frustration, sweat and agony. "That is my way," says the Bay.

An air of expectation instills the souls of men attempting to earn their daily bread from the waters of the Bay. It's a moody Bay. Sometimes gentle as a lamb and then quickly changing to a roaring lion waiting for the unwary to make a mistake and feel its terrible wrath.

The Bay seems to say, " I'm the master of your destiny. I reward those who I want. Sometimes I give a feast and sometimes I give just enough. And then Sometimes, nothing at all."

Never take me for granted. That's when I lash out at the complacent and offer only small catches and moody waters.

What will the Bay yield this day? Will it be bounty or will it be like taking bread from a hungry beggar who clings with a hand reluctant to let go? Only the Bay and time can answer that question.

Crab floats of many colors fill the waters, marking each man's personal property. Will the Bay yield its treasure? Sometimes she reluctantly releases her bounty, teasing man with promises of what might be. Promises that the next pot might be filled with Blue Beauties, lures man on and on.

Will the moody waters release what it holds deep in a protective grasp? Or will the audacity of man be his downfall?

There's debt for boat, bait and crew. Will the baskets be filled this day? Only the Bay holds the answer to that question. Seek and find the answer!

It is often said that he who works on the water is the greatest of gamblers, maybe close to a fool. Truly, he gambles on the weather, catch, trouble free operation of boat and equipment and the biggest gamble of all is the market. How much can he get from a bushel of treasure plucked from the moody waters of the Bay?

A large catch of the Blue Treasure means low prices, small catches, big prices. The cycle goes on and on. A struggle to catch, to sell, to reap and gain is an age- old game.

Dreams of large catches and, large sums of money earned are like a mirage that vanishes before men's eyes. Yet men continue the dream of what once was, but can never be again. Oh foolish Waterman, why do you struggle to reap a return from what you haven't sown?

Do you have the audacity to think you can win against me?

Labor on and keep dreaming an impossible dream. Maybe I will reward your effort, and again, maybe I won't. You dream of being independent, working on the water and answerable to no one but yourself. The truth is that I am your master. I decide success or ruin. Oh mortal man, how foolish of you to take me for granted. So says the Bay.

James Milton Hanna 2007

Chapter 1

Port Penn

Port Penn, Delaware was founded in 1763 and named in honor of either William Penn or his brother Richard. This small village located on the Delaware River along Route 9, once held promise of being a well-known port town. Many things favored the early settlers. They had a natural harbor, a road — of a sort — which ran from Port Penn to the Chesapeake Bay, and there was an abundance of freshwater marshes filled with muskrats which were trapped for both meat and fur, and there were fish, oysters and waterfowl in abundance.

To the west of Port Penn there was fertile farmland for those desiring to earn their livelihood from farming. However, when the Chesapeake-Delaware Canal opened in 1829 and the railroad in 1858, the dream of Port Penn becoming a large and busy port city was forever shattered.

Port Penn became a hub for muskrat trapping, oyster harvesting, sturgeon netting, and fishing for shad, weakfish and perch. The marshes were noted for the thousands of ducks that migrated there each fall.

Interpretive Center at Port Penn
The old Port Penn school house is an interesting place to visit. It contains a museum of the Port Penn area. The wooden carving standing in front of the center was made to honor watermen.

Many who worked on the water during the spring and summer became guides for hunters from Wilmington, Philadelphia and many other cities in the United States who enjoyed duck hunting. Many of the hunters the men guided were well-to- do and gave generous tips at the end of successful hunts. The guides took great pride in their expertise in calling ducks and geese. To a few, carving and selling decoys became a profitable occupation.

The economy of the area was based upon nature's bounty. Generations of men and boys followed their fathers working on the water. Working on the water is a hard occupation and far from a normal 8-5 workday. These men became known as Watermen. Many earned large incomes compared to those not working on the water. There were so many ducks in the area that many people living near the marsh were kept awake from the noise of the thousands of ducks spending the night on the marsh. Before strict game laws were enforced, many enjoyed eating ducks year round.

A trappers shack with a day's catch of muskrats.
(Photo: Port Penn Interpretive Center)

Display of animals once much sought after by Port Penn trappers Mink, Muskrat and traps used to catch these animals.
(Photo: Port Penn Interpretive Center)

Many youngsters spent time in the summer wading and boating with flat bottom boats. They used nets with long handles to catch young ducks that hadn't developed the ability to fly. This addition to the table was always welcomed. The half-grown ducks were tender and considered delicious. During the celebration of July fourth, thousands of these young mallards and black ducks were captured. There seemed to be an endless supply of ducks in the marshes.

A large number of men became market hunters and slaughtered untold thousands of ducks that were then taken to large cities and sold to restaurants — waterfowl was once part of their menu — and peddled door-to-door in residential areas. People's tastes were more attuned to wild flesh than today's generations. Oysters were a big part of the diet of people living near the shore. Oysters were canned, smoked or pickled to preserve that delicacy for later consumption in the winter months. This shellfish was stewed, fried, baked or eaten raw on the shell. No stuffing was without oysters. Oysters were the big money making treasure from the Bay. That ended in the nineteen hundred and fifties when disease killed off most of Delaware Bay oysters.

Market hunting came to an end in 1918 with the introduction of new Federal Game Laws. Thereafter, market hunting was done mostly at night and the kill sold with caution. All market hunting became illegal, but many couldn't resist the temptation of following a lifelong occupation. Many couldn't resist following in the footsteps of their fathers. Maybe they thought that the supply of ducks was unlimited.

A fishing shack mounted on boat
(Photo: Port Penn Interpretive Center)

Many of the market hunters deployed a set- up for hunting with the objective of killing large rafts of floating ducks and geese. The punt gun used was homemade and of a large caliber, having a much larger barrel than the 12 & 10 gauge shotguns of that day. Some punt guns were large enough to require one quarter pound of black powder and five pounds of lead shot — to save money, many collected roofing nails, small nuts and bolts to use in the guns — to send a deadly spray of destruction among large rafts of ducks. Often several dozen would be killed with one shot and a large number wounded.

Market hunting slowly died because law enforcement became more concentrated on those that illegally hunted and sold waterfowl. Since hunt-

Two youth proudly displaying fish they caught. About 1920. (Photo: Port Penn Interpretive Center)

ing migrating waterfowl came under Federal Law, that dampened the enthusiasm of the most ardent market hunter. Wherever former market hunters gathered, they would talk about the good old days and how unfair it was for the government to limit how many waterfowl they could kill, and worse of all, limiting when the waterfowl could be hunted. Even today, some still shoot for the market not only waterfowl, but also deer

Venison is still on the menu of many well-known restaurants and in the freezers of venison lovers. Some people pride themselves with eating venison year round and aren't above spotlighting deer—very illegal with severe penalties for those apprehended—late at night.

A number of men supplimented their income by collecting snapper turtles to sell to restaurants to cook their well-known "Snapper Soup." There seemed to always be a market for the turtles they caught and that holds true for these modern times. Snapper soup is delicious. Turtle hunters are called "Proggers" because of the method used to locate snappers. A long rod with a point and hook on each end is used to probe the mud alongside a pond or stream and locate a snapper in hibernation. When the hook catches the edge of the turtle's shell, it is dug from the mud. Today's "Proggers" mostly use wire traps for capturing turtles.

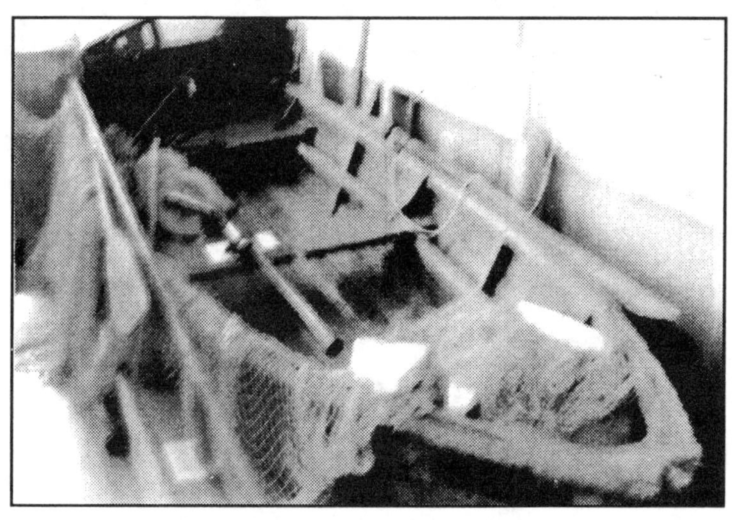

Type of boat used by early net fisherman.

Port Penn once sported a track for auto racing. The racetrack became famous because many noted auto racers of that day raced at the Port Penn track. Supposedly, it was at the Port Penn Racetrack that the first women drove race cars in the United States. In addition, a canning factory, located across the road from the old school building (Interpretive Center) operated for many years. The cannery as well as the race-track furnished employment to many people not working on the water.

George Constant holds a "Punt" gun once used by market hunters.

Port Penn residents once prided themselves with having an exceptionally good baseball team. That team was once considered the best in Delaware. Many small towns once had ball teams that played all over the state. Port Penn was at one time a very busy small village. Today, when driving through Port Penn, it is hard to believe all the activity that once took place there. Years ago when someone said he or she was from Port Penn, people would associate Port Penn with a lot of activity. Today, many people have no idea about Port Penn's past and what a busy small village it once was. Port Penn's fame has faded with time.

Like many small towns, the world seemed to have passed it by, with its past glory being only a faint memory to many of the older generation.

Chapter 2

The Dilemma

The two men woke from a deep sleep by the rocking of the trapper's shack they were in that sat atop two old boats. Many trappers of that time near Port Penn and Delaware City trapped for a living on large sections of marsh. Places to trap were highly contested and passed down from father to son. Muskrats, both the flesh and pelts were in demand. This insured a good income from five months intense labor, and then after the trapping season ended, the season for fishing would begin.

In several areas the small trapper's shacks were mounted on old boats and towed to a stream near where they trapped. The shacks were used for trapping and for fishing. The shacks would be equipped with a wood/coal stove, at least two cots and tables for skinning and eating. There would be two or three old chairs, a large barrel of fresh drinking water and a small supply of food, including plenty of coffee. And, most important to most of the trappers were several bottles of whiskey for therapeutic purposes. When they returned from checking their traps and finished the laborious task of skinning and stretching the catch, a large glass of whiskey would relax their tired aching bodies. There was an attic accessible by a ladder where they stored their furs to dry. They would visit their families about once a week, and sometimes a family member would come for a visit.

The fortunate trappers who lived next to a marsh where they trapped still needed a shack or utilized part of a barn for skinning muskrats and storing the pelts in the attic for drying until a fur buyer came by to purchase the trapper's catch.

One well-known trapper was a Mrs. Catherine Fox, (One of her relatives named his oyster boat "Catherine Fox" in her honor), who owned a thousand-acre marsh in the Port Penn area. She died in 1939. She had been widowed when still a young lady. She elected to continue operating the farm and trapping the marsh. Most years she would catch in excess of 10,000 muskrats. She became very apt grading muskrat pelts and developed a market for the meats of the muskrats. Most people in that area ate muskrat meat. She could sell the meat for 25-50 cents. That was a fair price back in the nineteen twenties and thirties.

As she aged it became difficult to walk the marshes trapping, so she started hiring other trappers to trap her marsh on a percentage basis. She knew muskrat trends and habits so well that she could tell when a trapper was either not trying very hard or was stealing from her. When upset, most didn't want to be around her and be a victim of her wrath.

Many fur buyers attempted to take advantage of

her because she was a woman and paid less than the pelts were worth so they could earn a higher profit. They soon discovered that she knew more about fur than they.

She became so disgusted with the local buyer that she refused to sell any of her pelts to them. About once a month a representative from a large fur buyer in New Jersey would come over to her home and buy her muskrat pelts at the price she placed on them. She never attempted to take advantage of these buyers and they treated her like a lady. To be invited to her farm for duck hunting and eating the delicious meals she served was a joy. Her muskrat and duck dinners were unequaled in any restaurant. People were careful to avoid saying or doing anything that would offend her. They didn't want to be excluded from her table. She was affectionately known as the "Muskrat Queen" of Delaware.

A movement of the shack woke the men from a deep sleep. Their cabin seemed to be rocking back and forth. One of the men thought the rocking was a result of drinking too much whiskey the previous evening. He staggered out of bed and thought that it was time to get up anyway. It was about 5 AM. He opened the door and stepped out of the cabin onto the boat to empty his bladder. What a surprise! They were no longer tied up to the poles they had driven into the mud to hold their shack in place at the edge of their marsh. They must have been at least a mile off shore moving fast with the out-going tide. Someone must have cut them loose!

That was a dirty trick to play on someone. It was

a cold morning, well below freezing and they were drifting without any means of propulsion. There was nothing they could do but hope a boat might come by and give them a tow back to their trapping area. Few boats would be out in the river or bay during that time of the year. They were truly in a desperate situation.

About noon they spotted a large boat approaching with a large column of black smoke boiling into the air. They quickly tied towels to trap poles and started waving their make- shift flags in the air to attract the attention of the fast approaching vessel. As the boat drew near they identified it as the *Thomas Clyde*, a well-known 310' ship, that made runs up and down the Bay all summer and an occasional trip in the winter.

The *Clyde* slowed and came to a stop about fifty feet from where they were. The mate asked them if they wanted to be taken aboard the *Clyde*. They were scared being on the water in a shack mounted on the unstable boats, but they had a few hundred dollars worth of fur stored in the attic, traps and other valuables that they didn't want to lose.

They answered that they wanted to stay on their shack and would the *Thomas Clyde's* Captain contact someone to tow them back up the Bay. The captain agreed and his small ship was soon only a speck in the distance.

Eventually the tide changed and they started drifting back up the river. Waves about two-feet high were breaking against the two boats that supported the shanty. At about three in the afternoon a thirty-five foot boat approached them. The occupants of the boat told them that he *Thomas Clyde* had stopped near them and asked if they would come up river and give the trappers in the floating shanty a tow. The trappers told the boat's crew that they definitely wanted a tow back to the stream near their trapping grounds. The boat crew asked a question that they also wanted answered: "How did you get in this predicament?"

After all it was a bit unusual to see a trapper's shack floating a couple of miles off shore without any means of propulsion. They wished they had the answer to that question too.

Examining the ropes that were used, to tie the boats holding the shanty in place, verified that they had indeed been cut. The boat shanty's supporting boats had drifted out into the river on an outgoing tide. That was really a mean trick to play on someone. Besides, both men had consumed three glasses of whiskey before going to bed just to relax them. They had been so relaxed that a herd of elephants could have charged by and they wouldn't have heard them.

When they arrived back to their marsh it was after dark. A full moon made it easy to locate their tie poles. After they were safely tied to their site, one of the men asked the owner of the boat that towed them, "What do we owe you?" The man told them that he disliked charging for helping them in their time of need. But gas cost fifteen cents a gallon and they didn't have much money, so the trappers could give them whatever they thought right. The only problem was that the trappers didn't have any cash on them. Finally, they decided to give the boat owner, who had towed them, several muskrat pelts valued at about twenty dollars along with half a bottle of adult beverage. That seemed to satisfy the boat's owner.

The next morning the men separated as usual to check the many traps set all over their marsh. They were surprised that they didn't catch very many muskrats in traps that hadn't been checked the day before. Maybe some one was stealing their caught muskrats.

The next morning when they went their separate ways checking traps, one of the men decided to check a ditch at the far edge of their trapping area. He discovered a strange boat tied up in that ditch. In the boat were a large number of muskrats and several of his own traps. Normally a trapper marked his traps so they could be identified if needed. The tide was starting to flow out. He took all the muskrats and his traps and then pushed the boat into the fast moving water where it would be taken out into the Delaware River. Carrying the muskrats and traps he walked back to the trapper's shanty and waited for his partner to arrive. No one had a right to be trapping their marsh and stealing muskrats and traps. Maybe what he had just done would teach the thief or maybe thieves a lesson.

When his partner finally came in he was evidently upset. "You know what happened to me," he stated in an angry voice. "I caught a man stealing from our traps. He had a burlap bag filled with muskrats. I yelled at him, and he dropped the bag and ran toward that ditch on the far side of our marsh. I couldn't catch him wearing these chest waders. He got completely away from me. At least he had dropped the bag of muskrats that he had taken from our traps. That man really could move fast across the marsh. I wish I would have had a shotgun with me. I could have made him move even faster with a load of birdshot in his butt."

A couple of days later another trapper dropped by for a glass of adult liquid refreshment and told them about a man from New Jersey who claimed to have lost his boat. The man had pounded on the door of the Faulk's farmhouse and asked for a ride to Delaware City. He was cold and very muddy. He was given the ride as he requested, but Mr. Faulk charged him five dollars for the ride, and for being awakened at two AM.

After that incident everything was normal for the rest of the season. Sometimes the men wondered what would have happened if the *Thomas Clyde* hadn't happened by on that cold December day.

Note: The *Thomas Clyde* went out of service in 1929 and was sunk as a breakwater in the Delaware River. It's still there under tons of rock.

Chapter 3

Collins Beach

Collins Beach is shown on county maps. Once a person drives to Collins Beach all that can be found is a parking lot and boat ramps. That wasn't the case back in the late 1800s. Collins Beach was once the best known resort on Delaware Bay.

Hundreds of people once flocked to Collins Beach for vacations and entertainment. Several boats serviced that busy resort. The *Thomas Clyde* was the best known boat that hauled passengers to and from major cities to Collins and Woodland Beaches. Most of the people vacationing at those resorts were from Philadelphia and Wilmington.

It is difficult to imagine when visiting Collins Beach that a large resort was once situated there. Once Collins Beach hosted a hotel, rental cottages and a large entertainment pier. About one hundred rental boats were available for those wishing to fish or have fun on the water. The hotel's restaurant served delicious food with specialties such as crab cakes, soup, baked shad and rockfish. Snapper soup and oysters fixed about anyway one wanted were on the menu.

Many well-to-do families owned summer cottages there or reserved cottages for their summer outing a year in advance. It was a vacationer's paradise.

On October, 1887, a hurricane moved up the coast and through Delaware. Those were the days before reliable weather forecasting was available. The storm came as a surprise. Winds of about seventy miles per hour swept across Delaware tearing roofs off many building and blowing trees down all over the state. Wilmington and the Delaware Bay were hard hit from that storm.

The main tourist season was over when the storm hit on that fateful night. A tidal wave — twelve feet above sea level — swept up Delaware Bay and changed forever the shoreline of the Bay. Collins Beach buildings were mostly destroyed or badly damaged along with the beautiful beach where happy throngs of people played and bathed in the sun. (One has to wonder how the vacationers coped with the swarms of Green Head Flies and mosquitoes for which the shore of Delaware Bay is noted).

The beach was divided into three sections. One was the ladies only beach, one was a men only beach and the other section was for families. Dress codes were strictly enforced. Men were required to wear a swimsuit covering their chests to below their knees. Women wore a swimsuit that covered from neck to ankles. If people back in those days could see how people dress at the beach today they would be shocked.

The storm breached the shoreline in many places and created new streams flowing into Delaware Bay and turned the large marshes from fresh water to salt-water marshes. Before the storm and accompanying tidal wave there was a large fresh water marsh near Collins Beach that was noted for large stands of White Cedar. The cedar trees were valuable for boat building and furniture. The inflow of salt water killed the many trees growing in the marsh. The storm was so devastating that the Collins Beach Resort was never completely rebuilt.

Up until 1903, and a change of ownership, people had attempted to restore the Beach to its former glory. Things were just not the same after the big storm. A book, *Ho! For Collins Beach*, written by E.D. Bryan, M.D. is a well-written history of Collins Beach.

Chapter 4

Market Hunters

Punt Guns and other Illegal Ways of Taking Game

Most people don't know what a Punt Gun is. Most have never heard the term Punt Gun. When people start talking about the past, especially those living around Delaware or the Chesapeake Bay with its large marshes, some will remember their fathers and grandfathers talking about the days of market hunting. For those who don't know, a Punt Gun is a large pipe 1" to 2" in diameter that has been modified with a trigger and hole for an ignition cap. The barrel had a length of about six to ten feet, and was attached on a swivel to a small boat. It is made like a small cannon. It is really an oversize shotgun. Usually the boat was a small flat scow that is easy to paddle.

Black powder was poured into the barrel or pipe and pieces of rags or paper are used for wadding to hold the powder in place. Next shotgun pellets or roofing nails — sometimes bolts and nuts — were packed into the barrel and rags are used to hold the shot in place. A long ramrod similar to that used when loading a black powder musket, but much larger, is used to pack the powder and shot tightly in the barrel.

The gun was often used at night to hunt large rafts of ducks or geese and also swans. The hunter would position the boat at the edge of an open body of water with the boat covered with marsh grass making it similar to a duck blind. The hunter would sometimes place decoys on the water and start calling ducks and geese. The hunter would lie flat in the boat and use two paddles the size of ping-pong paddles to maneuver the boat. The objective was to get positioned near where large numbers of waterfowl were floating. The goal was to find a large flock of ducks or geese so that one shot would dispatch large numbers. Once the makeshift guns were fired large numbers of waterfowl would be killed and large numbers wounded.

Often the hunter would have a good retriever, maybe a Labrador or a Chesapeake Bay Retriever, to catch the many wounded birds. In a single night in the autumn a hunter, using a Pont Gun, could kill several hundred fowl.

Early the next morning, after a successful hunt, the hunter would take his kill to Wilmington or Philadelphia to certain restaurants that bought and offered wild game on their menu. There was also a good market for ducks and geese in peddling the waterfowl door to door in housing developments.

By 1918, Federal Game Laws were created outlawing using the punt gun and market hunting. There is always a segment of the population that doesn't appreciate having to adhere to new laws restricting their outdoor activities. Many depended on market hunting as a good part of their livelihood. They fished, trapped muskrats, captured Snapper Turtles, dredged oysters and crabbed as a means of earning a living. Selling waterfowl was a big part of the income of many watermen of yore.

Despite the new waterfowl laws that outlawed punt guns and selling waterfowl, many still followed that occupation. They had to be crafty in their activities. Before the new laws were enacted some used a punt gun in daytime as well as at night. Working at night in remote ditches and coves, a large number of hunters still continued to operate. They had to be very careful not to get caught. It is difficult to believe the large numbers of ducks of all species that once spent time on the Bay or in the marshes adjacent to the Bay.

Some market hunters still pursued the occupation of market hunter into and through the Great Depression. There were some incidents of using too much powder and the punt guns exploding. Some hunters were hurt badly and other hunters became careful in measuring the exact amount of powder to propel the shot several hundred yards.

Some hunters were so good at their occupation that they earned equal to a week's salary from one night's work. The days where there were endless flocks of ducks are only a memory to a few who have lived to an old age. If you happen to meet an old fellow that lived around the Bay and Marshes in the old days, ask him what he knows of the olden days of duck hunting.

You might be surprised when he gets a dreamy look in his eyes and starts telling stories of those days of so long ago when market hunters lived and plied their skills.

Many people who worked the water and marshes relied on their own "tricks of the trade." Muskrat trappers in the heydays of trapping and earning a living from trapping those little bundles of fur and edible meat used many ways to capture the little critters.

In an attempt to maximize the catch of muskrats, some enterprising trappers developed a special trap that would catch and drown large numbers of muskrats. Such a trap was made from "chicken wire" and was about six feet long. It was roughly ten inches in diameter. Each end of the trap had a funnel that the "rats would swim into and would be unable to swim back out and therefore would drown. The trap was set in runs or trails that showed lots of use. It was submersed and once the muskrat enter it was hopelessly trapped.

People have been known to catch ten or twelve muskrats in one night from a single funnel trap. The traps had to be moved often to different locations to prevent catching all the muskrats in that area and to assure leaving seed for the following year. The funnel trap has been outlawed for at least 60 years.

Other trappers started "snooze" trapping. This type of trapping was nothing more than a wire noose tied to a stick and placed in muskrat runs or entrances to muskrat houses or dens. The advantage of such a trap was the ease of setting it, the low cost of wire and the lighter weight. Traps were more costly and a bag of traps carried across the marsh could get heavy as the trapper collected his catch and often struggled through deep mud. The trapper could make up a bunch of snares and carry them in his coat pocket and attached to a stick once he decided where to make a set. Such sets are illegal in Delaware, but knowing some of the older trappers, I would bet that this type of trap is still used.

When geese would pass through migrating south each year, they would only stop in Delaware a short time before flying on to North and South Carolina each fall. Some enterprising trappers would drill holes in corn grains and tie a strong cord through the hole and leave about three feet of line attached. Stakes were then driven into the ground and the cord tied to the stake. Several such sets were made and corn sprinkled liberally over and around the corn tied to the cords. Geese would land in the fields at night to feed and start eating the corn left by the trapper. Once a goose swallowed one of the grains of corn with the cord attached, it was hopelessly trapped. Of course, taking geese in that manner is highly illegal and if a person got caught using that technique, there would be a big fine and maybe some jail time.

In the 1920s, long raccoon coats were the rage. Raccoon prices rose sharply and the trappers concentrated on that animal. Many started using hounds to chase the raccoon until it came to bay up a tree. The hunter would use a spotlight to locate the raccoon so it could be shot.

Some trappers purchased telephone linemen's

climbing gear. They would walk through woodlands bordering streams until they found a large, hollow tree. Raccoon trees would have the bark worn smooth from the animals climbing up and down the tree to their holes. The trapper would climb the tree up to where the den entrance was located. He would shine a flash-light into the hole and once a raccoon was located, shoot the animal in the head. One trapper that used this method of killing raccoon told me that once he killed 5 raccoons in one den. Obviously, this is illegal under present game laws.

The old Daniel Boone series on Television back in the fifties and sixties created another boom for raccoon fur. Everyone just had to have a coon skin hat like Daniel Boone wore. Combined with the demand for raccoon fur and an epidemic of distemper and rabies almost wiped out raccoon in North and South Carolina back in the late 1960s and early 1970s.

The government sponsored a program to trap raccoon in Delaware and ship them to the Carolinas. Several trappers in Delaware gained contracts from the government and captured a few hundred. That was the first time in their years of trapping that they ever thought of catching raccoon alive rather than killing and skinning that creature. A building on the Bombay Hook preserve was used to store raccoon in cages until they could be shipped to the Carolinas. One night a large number got loose in the building where they were confined in cages. The men had a difficult time recapturing the mischievous little creature. Raccoon were in the rafters and every nook and cranny they could find.

Chapter 5

Slaughter Beach

Slaughter Beach is a small community first settled in 1681 as a whaling station and located near the mouth of the Mispillion River that flows from Milford.

There seems to be a problem discovering how Slaughter Beach got its name. I asked several people if they knew why the area was named Slaughter Beach. I was really surprised at the various answers I received.

One man said that he remembered someone telling him that a large slaughterhouse was situated in that area at one time, so it was appropriately named Slaughter Beach. That sounded feasible, but then I asked another person the same question and the reply I received was "There was once a battle between Indians and the early settlers and the Indians were slaughtered. That is why it's called Slaughter Beach."

Not to be outdone was a man who thought that a family named Slaughter once owned the surrounding area. Then another person told me that the name of the village came from a market hunter killing a large number of ducks using a "punt" gun back in the early days of market hunting. He had killed several hundred ducks in one moonlit night. That had really been a slaughter.

Perhaps the most feasible answer to the question regarding how Slaughter Beach got its name was from Bill Rafter, a resident of the area. He and his wife, Rose, operate the Slaughter Beach Mini-Mart. He was told by some of the old timers that in the early days that area had been a whaling station. He thinks that the whaling station was once located near the site of the present fire station. Maybe the whalers had a good season to call it "slaughter" and that name stuck.

For years not too many people lived there. The population increased during the 1920s, 30s, 40s and then ballooned to its present population. Many people from Milford and other inland towns built cottages there to escape the heat of the summers. It was a good place for the wife and children to spend the summer during the oppressing hot humid days. Also, during that time a terrible and dreaded disease, Polio, was crippling many people across the nation. Young children and young adults seemed to be more affected. At the beach it was about ten degrees cooler and there was the Bay for wading and swimming to keep cool.

The Amy constructed a fort in 1917 near Slaughter Beach for coastal defense. It was named Fort Saulsbury in honor of Willard Saulsbury, a former Senator from Delaware.

The U.S Department of Defense thought that an enemy warship might sail up Delaware Bay and destroy both Philadelphia and Wilmington and interrupt shipping through the Chesapeake-Delaware Canal.

Two 12" guns were mounted and various facilities were constructed to support the troops stationed there. Several bunkers are still remaining.

A boardwalk several hundred yards long once ran along the shore in front of the cottages. (Photo courtesy of Mrs. Minner who spent her summers as a child at Slaughter Beach.)

The batteries were named after prominent military leaders who fought in the Revolutionary War. Like the guns mounted at Pea Patch Island over seventy years before, the guns were never fired in anger. During World War II the guns were removed and the facility turned into a camp for German prisoners of war. Many older folk remember the German prisoners of war confined there. The prisoners were well treated and allowed to work on farms under guard. They weren't considered a threat and most likely the prisoners realized how fortunate they were to be out of the war.

There were some interesting incidents created by

German prisoners. One evening two prisoners failed to return from working on a farm. Apparently the guards hadn't counted and realized the prisoners were missing. The two prisoners walked to Milford and into a bar and ordered beer. They spoke excellent English and the bartender didn't realize they were prisoners. They had removed the jackets that had POW written across the back and were wearing only tee shirts and jeans. After they were well intoxicated, they told the bartender to call the authorities at Fort Saulsbury to come and pick them up. "We are German prisoners of war and we need a ride back to the Fort." That incident was really an embarrassment to those men working at the Fort.

Another incident occurred at a farm near Milford. Prisoners harvested potatoes and other crops from surrounding farms and were paid a small amount to be used for toilet items, soda and other snacks. One prisoner climbed into a large truck and started driving at breakneck speed around the potato field. He refused to stop, so the guards blocked the only exit from the field and the prisoner drove the truck at a high speed around in circles until it ran out of gas. He meekly surrendered and was taken back to the Fort. His punishment was one week of working in the dining hall doing all the dirty work such as scrubbing pots and pans. Also, he was required to peel potatoes for all 300 prisoner's meals. Sad to say, American prisoners of war weren't treated well by the Germans and Japanese. The Germans treated their prisoners much better than the Sons of Nippon did those they held.

Fort Saulsbury was sold to private interests in 1948.

I'm grateful to Mrs. Annie Townsend Minner for writing to me and enclosing a picture of her and several friends sitting on the boardwalk. Yes, there was once a large boardwalk that stretched for several hundred yards along the shore. A pier three or four hundred feet long stretched out into the Bay. It was a delightful place to spend the summer. Her memories of spending the summers in the late thirties and into the forties at Slaughter Beach are indeed cherished.

She remembered her father making a float from old metal barrels and building a platform on it and then anchoring it a few yards off shore so that at high tide people would be able use the "Floating Island" for sun bathing and diving. She remembers kids placing sails on wagons and "sailing" all the way down the boardwalk. At one time there was a hotel, a general store and dance hall at Slaughter Beach. The area has been hit by several hurricanes during the twentieth century.

During and after prohibition — the 1920s and 1930s — Rumrunners often operated out of the Mispillion River and surrounding areas. Residents would, often in the stillness of the night, hear the roar of speeding boats and occasionally, the chatter of machinegun fire coming from out in the Bay. One particular incident that a father told his son about was when he lived at Slaughter Beach as a young man. He said it wasn't unusual for the Revenuer's boats to chase boats loaded with whiskey along Slaughter Beach and into the Mispillion River.

One story is that of a very daring rumrunner who had motor problems while attempting, in the wee hours of the morning, to evade a Revenue boat that was in hot pursuit. He was a mile or two ahead of the pursuing boat. Seeing that outrunning the boat was impossible, he anchored a hundred yards off Slaughter Beach and tossed the twenty cases of whiskey he was hauling overboard. He turned on the boat's lights, lit a lantern, and grabbed a fishing pole and started fishing.

The Government boat came roaring up and circled the area using a searchlight in an attempt to locate the boat they were chasing. Finally they motored near where the man was fishing and asked him if he had seen another boat in the area. "No I haven't, mine is the only boat here. I'm just trying to catch a good mess of trout. However, they aren't biting very well," he told them. He didn't bother to tell them that he had no bait on the hook.

One of the men from the Government boat asked if he would give permission for them to search his boat. He told them he didn't mind at all. A quick look around by one of the deck hands failed to locate any alcoholic beverage. It was 2 AM, but back in those days overnight fishing was enjoyed by a large number of fishermen. Night fishing was much cooler than fishing on a hot day. Most fishermen knew that fish fed closer to shore at night. Sometimes night fishermen would anchor in the Bay and suspend a strong light over the water near their boat. The light would attract insects and the insects would attract fish. Some even claimed having dipped trout from the water with a net.

The Government boat immediately departed in search of the evasive boat they had been chasing. The men aboard the Government boat reasoned that the Rumrunner had fled up the Mispillion River. Attempting to locate a boat hiding in one of the guts flowing into the river would be impossible, especially at night. There was always a danger of running aground in the river with their larger boat.

At low tide the next morning several men drove as near the beach as possible and waded out into the water feeling with their feet for cases of whiskey. They located most of the cases, loaded them on an old truck, covered everything with hay and left the area to haul the whiskey to Philadelphia.

Several times later in the year when people were seining for fish with a net in that area they would occasionally bring in a bottle of Canadian Whiskey. Seining was a big thing in the olden days. Large nets several hundred yards long would be dropped overboard from a small boat and teams of oxen or horses would pull the nets onto the shore. The fish were sold or else pickled in brine or smoked for later use.

Running illegal whiskey was even more of a problem on the New Jersey side of the Bay. There were many more rivers and hiding places for the Rumrunners to evade the Government boats. After all, a man who had worked the rivers, creeks, and marshes for years found it easy to evade boats chasing them in their own back yard. They knew all the side guts leading from the main streams and the best hiding places.

One man told me that after one "Big Blow" several cottages were damaged and sand was pushed to a depth of four feet covering the road that runs behind the cottages. All that sand was bulldozed back onto the beach and in the process covered the boardwalk. It was never rebuilt. If a person wanted to start digging through the sand most likely a part of the boardwalk could be found buried and preserved under the sand.

That area was, for several generations, a great fishing area. The large parking lot was once filled with pickups and boat trailers. Now on most days only a few trucks with boat trailers are parked in this parking facility. The 1970s and 80s were good for fishing. Several watermen still work out of the Mispillion River and Slaughter Beach. Pilot boats are stationed there and take pilots back and forth to ships making their way up the Bay to Wilmington, Philadelphia and through the Delaware-Chesapeake Canal into the Chesapeake Bay and Baltimore.

Bill Rafter once lived in Newark before moving to the Slaughter Beach area. He was an avid fisherman and spent most of his spare time each summer fishing on Delaware Bay and often launched his boat at Slaughter Beach.

One day, he and a friend, William Thomas of Smyrna, were fishing about a mile off shore from the mouth of the Mispillion River near buoy "A" when Thomas hooked a weakfish (Trout). He was using a 17-pound test line with a yellow buck tail and purple worm, with a strip of squid attached for extra attraction. The fish gave him quite a fight and finally after landing the big fish, Thomas realized that he might have a record catch for Delaware Bay. The weakfish was 37-1/2 inches long (many weakfish that length have been caught from Delaware Bay, but what made the difference was the girth of the fish) and 21-1/2 inches in girth.

The previous weakfish caught by hook and line in Delaware Bay weighed 17 pounds, 12 ounces. Thomas' weakfish weighed 19 pounds and 2 ounces. Not only was the catch a record for Delaware Bay, but it exceeded a 19 pound fish caught in the Chesapeake Bay. This marvelous catch may have tied or exceeded the world record for weakfish caught on hook and line. To other fishermen, ... "eat your hearts out in envy. Keep fishing and maybe one of these days you will beat that record."

May 27, 1989 is a day that many who fished on Delaware Bay will never forget. That was the day of the big storm that swept across the Bay in two different waves causing over twenty-foot high waves. A big fishing tournament involving over 150 boats was underway that day. Plus, many other boaters were fishing in different areas of the Bay. The first indication anyone had of an impending storm was an announcement from the Coast Guard over the radio for all boats to immediately leave the Delaware Bay.

One boater looked back toward the Delaware side of the Bay and saw a huge wall of dark clouds rushing toward where he was located. He and a friend were in his 25' boat and usually felt safe when the Bay was rough. He quickly turned the boat around and gave it full throttle toward the Jersey side of the Bay hoping to outrun the approaching storm. Suddenly, the sky ahead of him darkened and the waves started growing to the most threatening waves he had ever experienced on the Bay. Later it was reported that the waves had grown to between 12-25 feet. Just imagine, being in a 25' boat and the waves reaching a height of 25'. Just the thought of being on the Bay with such adverse weather conditions is scary.

During this storm two or three people lost their lives and many more were thrown into the water when their boats capsized.

Cedar Creek

Many boaters were saved by seeking shelter behind large tankers anchored awaiting pilots or smaller vessels to lighten their cargo before proceeding up the Bay. That storm was an unbelievable nightmare for anyone boating on Delaware Bay that day.

Mr. Rafter and his fishing companion struggled through the entire storm in an effort to prevent being swamped or capsized. The boat owner related that the only thing saving them was his fishing partner who was an old Navy man who had experienced such storms in other parts of the world in a small boat and knew how to keep the boat afloat.

Another nightmarish experience that a few people boating on the water have endured, is that of waterspouts. One young man related that he was up the Bay north of Port Mahon when he observed a large waterspout roaring down the Bay toward him. He immediately turned south in an effort to outrun the approaching waterspout. To his chagrin it seemed to be gaining on his boat. He changed course to get out of the path of the approaching storm but it seemed to follow him. By that time interest, then fascination had turned to almost panic. It seemed that the storm had a mind of its own and was attempting to catch him. Just as suddenly as it had appeared it vanished into the sky leaving him shaken. People read about waterspouts appearing in the open sea but it is difficult to imagine one in the Delaware Bay.

It is hard to truly envision what villages like Slaughter Beach were once like. Get some older people from that area tell about when they were young and lived at Slaughter Beach. Most will get a dreamy look in their eyes as they tell about the wonderful times they had at Slaughter Beach. The fishing was unbelievably good and the place would be crowded in the summer with all kinds of activities taking place. It was the place for a family to be during the long hot summers before air conditioning.

Chapter 6

Pirates on Delaware Bay

"The Golden Age of Piracy 1650-1720"

Delaware Bay's history of use by settlers in the New World is indeed old. Legends persist of pirates and treasure being associated with the Bay. Such names as Captain Kidd, Black Beard, and many others who were pirates turn up from time to time. Many efforts have been made to find treasure supposedly buried along the coast of Delaware Bay. And if any treasure has been found, the finders have kept it a secret. One fact that is known is that many poor families have suddenly apparently become financially secure without anyone knowing where their good fortune came from. That was before income tax and filing annual tax returns. Could they have discovered pirate loot or maybe bootlegged whiskey?

Early one dawn, a ship mounting about thirty guns was observed anchored in Lewes Harbor. This stately ship was flying the Dutch flag, a country that at that time was an ally of Great Britain. On numerous occasions foreign ships put in at Lewes for various reasons.

Some for repairs from damage received from a storm in the Atlantic, damage from pirates, to replenish water and supplies or to trade with the several trading houses in Lewes Town, as Lewes was called back in those days.

Obviously this ship wasn't a routine cargo ship. It had a well- kept look and was a handsome ship and most likely French made. A boat was soon seen approaching the dock. The boat contained six men manning the oars. Two more well dressed men were seated in the bow of the boat. The two men in the bow were let off at the dock and the boat returned to the ship.

The two men were heavily tanned, well dressed and sported a gold ear-ring in one ear. The clothing they wore was that worn by the gentry of that era. Their overall appearance was that of successful men. The men saw a sign hanging above the door of a tavern near the wharf and entered. The sign read "The Boars Head Inn." They moved to the rear and took seats at a table in the corner. The barmaid anticipated a good tip from such well-dressed men and hurried over and took their order for ale, meat and bread. The men were pleasant and made casual conversation with the young girl. They asked her about the trading merchants operating near the tavern.

"If you had goods to sell, which merchant would you try to sell to?" they asked the girl.

"Oh, that's easy to answer," she told them. "Martin Wicks is always buying and selling about anything he can get his hands on. He's a nice man and comes in here each day to break his fast. He always leaves a good tip," she said with a giggle.

Martin Wicks looked up when the bell rang indicating someone was entering his place of business. The two men entering were well dressed, armed with a customary cutlass and each had a pistol stuck in their sashes under the cloaks each wore. Their dress was indicative of ship officers. One of the men introduced himself as Edward Teach. He was a large man with a long, neatly trimmed black beard.

His eyes were as black as his beard. There was a toughness about him that immediately drew attention. He seemed the type of man who usually got his way. This visit started a relationship that spanned several years. The man had goods to sell and he wanted Wicks to be his agent. No long drawn out introduction, just getting down to business without any fanfare.

The man named Teach told the businessman that he was the Captain of a Privateer, duly authorized by the Crown to raid enemy ships, mostly Spanish in the Caribbean. He showed the merchant papers with the seal of the crown affixed. Everything looked legal to Wicks. After some discussion, he agreed to handle all goods left on consignment, and put aside monies due to Captain Teach. Teach told the merchant that he or a representative would make infrequent trips to Lewes Town to bring more goods. With each trip they would settle their account.

Later in the day, boat after boat moved from the ship to the dock and back. The goods were taken to Wicks warehouse by several men he hired anytime a ship arrived bringing goods for him to sell. The boats returning to the ship carried casks of food, water, sides of bacon and pickled beef and all the gunpowder that could be purchased in Lewes Town. With the outgoing tide the ship slowly moved out into the Bay and into the Atlantic and into history.

That visit was the start of several years of the Wick's company dealing with Black Beard the pirate or his representatives.

Mr. Wicks in later years stated that, "He didn't know the man he was dealing with was the notorious Black Beard the pirate."

The Wicks Company earned a small fortune fencing the famous pirate's loot.

The pirate became such a scourge that the Colonial Government set a price on his head and a naval officer, Lt. Maynard was assigned two vessels and crew with the purpose of tracking down Black Beard. The crafty pirate ran circles around Lt. Maynard's ships. Unfortunate for Black Beard, Maynard was like a hound on the scent of a hare. He kept on and on in his pursue of the pirate. On several occasions he missed him by a few days. He and some of his crew would go ashore in small port towns along the Carolinas and hang around the taverns listening for bits of information that they might gain from gossip and talk from drunken sailors. Most sailors enjoyed getting drunk and many couldn't help boasting of their activities.

On night they struck pay dirt. Some of the pirates were in a tavern drinking when one let slip that they had to get back to the ship soon or Teach would be mad, and they didn't want to upset that mean old buzzard.

The men, followed by Lt. Maynard and two of his men, pushed off from the dock in a row boat and started down stream toward several islands in that North Carolina Bay. Lt. Maynard ordered two of his men to follow the pirates at a distance in another boat while he returned to his ships and got underway. Maynard's two small ships slowly moved down stream in the direction the pirates had gone. Soon he sighted the men he had sent to follow the pirates frantically rowing against the tide toward his ship. He took them and the boat aboard. They cautioned him that the pirate ship was about one-half mile away anchored near an island. Tall trees on the island hid the pirate ship's masts from view until within a short distant of the island.

Lt. Maynard anchored his ship behind another island and made plans to attempt seizing the pirate ship. He and thirty sailors armed themselves with cutlasses, flintlock pistols and a few muskets. Each man carried a knife of personal choice. They selected early morning and hopefully, a fog, to silently row three boats to the anchored ship. Surprising the pirates gave them the only hope for overcoming the odds of fighting against skilled men who were well acquainted with warfare on the water. Lieutenant Maynard was sure that the pirates would feel secure and wouldn't be on guard so early in the morning. He assumed, and correctly too, that most of the pirates had been to their cups most of the night. Their favorite drink was strong rum.

At dawn, fog dropped visibility to about fifty yards. They were able to approach within several yards of the ship before they separated with one boat approaching the pirate ship from the far side and the two remaining boats approaching the ship at bow and stern. Everything went unbelievably well and they were able to scramble aboard the ship with drawn cutlasses. One man was on watch, somewhat drunk, and not fully awake. He was soon dispatched and fell with a thump to the deck.

The main cabin door sprung open and Black Beard stepped on the deck with a cutlass in one hand and a pistol in the other. He quickly shot the man nearest Lt. Maynard and leaped toward the raiding party. The sound of his pistol being discharged brought most of his crew charging onto the deck. Maynard engaged in hand to hand combat with Black Beard and after a short struggle, the noted pirate died at the hands of Lt. Maynard.

He ended the life of one of the terrors of the sea. The rest of Black Beard's crew quickly surrendered and two weeks later were hung. After the demise of Captain "Blackbeard" Edward Teach, other pirates were more than willing to fill his shoes. However, it was difficult to surpass the notoriety that Edward Teach had achieved.

An infamous pirate who preceded Edward Teach was Captain Kidd who also had connections with Delaware Bay.

Captain Kidd was a good friend of the Governor of New York. Kidd had several years' experience as a ship's captain and had established a good reputation. He was selected to captain a small Man- of- War ship to be used as a privateer on the high seas against England's enemies, France and Spain. Operating a Privateer could be highly profitable. A Captain operating under license as a Privateer was nothing more than a legal pirate. Sometimes it seemed that the Privateer's Captains had a difficult time distinguishing which vessels were friendly or enemies of the Crown. The quote, "dead men tale no tales" often applied. No survivors were allowed by some of the pirates. Many had heard of Captain Teaches' fate and didn't want anyone to live and testify against them

Captain Kidd manned his ship with a crew of mixed nationalities. Many were deadbeats from the waterfront that somehow escaped the pressing crews from the British Man-of-Wars. England was at war with France and Spain and had a difficult time finding crewmen for His Majesty's ships. The government welcomed the Privateers because they could attack cargo ships flying the flag of Spain or France and free their Man-of-War front line ships for fighting England's enemies. During that period, two or three cruises by a Privateer could result in wealth beyond expectation. The spoils were divided into three parts: the owner of the ship received fifty percent, the captain twenty-five percent and the remaining twenty-five percent divided among the crew.

The Privateer, Captain Kidd, won his wings as a full-scale pirate after an incident at sea when he attacked and sank a ship from a neutral country. He was having very bad fortune on that cruise because of not being able to locate an enemy ship to plunder. His crew was about to mutiny because there had been promises of riches to be made and expectations were high. The entire trip had been a failure. They hadn't sighted a single enemy ship and had suffered through several bad storms and were becalmed for many days. They had been at sea for two months and hadn't earned any money whatsoever from attacking other ships. Finally, Captain Kidd succumbed to pressure from his crew and overtook and plundered a neutral ship. After looting the ship, he destroyed all of the ship's boats and set powder charges to sink the merchant ship with all hands and passengers. He knew that dead men told no tales.

Captain Kidd sailed away from the doomed ship seeking another ship to prey on. Aboard the ship was a prominent man from England who had once met Kidd at a reception in London. That man, his wife, the Captain and a few of the crew constructed a raft and survived the sinking. They were later picked up by an English Man-of-War and transported to England. Their testimony officially outlawed Captain Kidd.

Kidd had previously made several trips up Delaware Bay to Wilmington and Philadelphia before becoming a pirate. He knew the area well. About a year after sinking the neutral ship, he sailed for New York with his ship filled with loot from ships he had captured. He needed to unload his ship, divide the spoils with his sponsor, the Governor of New York, and settle with his crew. However, by that time he had become a pirate at heart. On the way up from the Caribbean to New York, he decided that he had worked too hard for all his plunder and didn't think he should have to give his sponsor half of the loot.

Captain Kidd sailed for the last time up Delaware Bay and went ashore near what is now the Leipsic River (Once known as Duck Creek) and is reputed to have buried several large chests filled with valuables such as silver plate, gold, and gems. Captain Kidd sailed from Delaware Bay to his final destiny in New York. On the way there he again stopped at Sandy Point, New Jersey and buried more treasure. He was shocked when he sailed into New York Harbor and instead of being welcomed by the Governor and congratulated for a successful voyage, he and his crew were arrested by the authorities and charged with piracy. Piracy was an hanging offence.

He attempted to bribe his one time friend, the Governor, to drop the charges against him. He told the Governor about the chests of treasure buried at Sandy Point, New Jersey. The treasure was recovered and Captain Kidd was still kept in irons and sent to England for trial and to meet his accusers—the Captain and passengers of the neutral ship he had sunk.

In order to save himself—he seemed to care less about what happened to his crew—he offered to reveal where other treasures were hidden, including a large treasure in Delaware Bay. The court sentenced Captain Kidd to hang and the sentence was immediately carried out. For many years, people have searched for the lost treasure and as far as is known, it was never found.

Delaware's coast-line was easily accessible to pirates. For a time, pirates raided all the way up the Bay and River to New Castle. Crews from ships anchored in deeper water, manned small boats and raided farms located near the water. Pirates who looted shops and homes located near the water also raided the town of Lewes. The town's people fled in terror when several boatloads of pirates rowed ashore armed with cutlass and pistols. No one resisted and the entire town fled at the sight of the "freebooters" from the sea.

To make matters worse for Delaware Bay, many young men dreamed of being a pirate. To them being a pirate meant that they could escape from a lifetime of toil on a farm. They dreamed of having money, good clothing, all the rum they wanted to consume, and of course women.

Many thought that being a pirate meant a life of adventure. Few stopped to realize that pirates were regularly caught and hung in many areas of the world. The average life of a pirate was very short.

Being a pirate is romanticized in books and stories told, but in truth there was little honor between pirates. They would even attack each other if there was a possibility of eliminating competition. In sum, a pirate's life was short and filled with danger. Many pirates who survived a lifetime of piracy often came ashore minus an eye, leg or arm. Many pirate chiefs had a pact with their crew whereby a crewmember who lost an arm, leg or eye would receive a certain sum of money and set ashore hear some village or small town.

Many young men who left the farm to become

pirates often wished they were back on the farm. Those who escaped execution did return to farm life and enjoyed in their later years telling stories about the time they served under the Black Flag.

At one time there were pirates who operated in the Delaware River and Delaware Bay. Philadelphia was a busy port and many young men would hear stories from ship's crews about the pirates in the Caribbean. A sailor's life was harsh at best. Many sailors day-dreamed of being a pirate. Their stories glorified being a pirate. The telling of pirate stories motivated many young men to be pirates on Delaware Bay because there was no way they could ever purchase a sea going vessel and sail to the Caribbean where the Spanish treasure ships operated. But, Delaware Bay was near and local pirates didn't need a large boat like would be needed at sea.

Many ships would travel up Delaware Bay to the Christina River to have their hulls careened. A ship's bottom covered with barnacles made a ship sail very slowly. Many pirates brought their ships to a shipyard on the Christina River to have work accomplished. Before coming up river to have their ships worked on, the pirates removed all evidence that would connect them to being buccaneers. Many people still wondered how the deckhands of such ships dressed so well and had so much money to spend on drink and wenches that hung around the inns.

Locating a twenty to thirty foot boat in the immediate area was must easier. They had the choice of stealing such a boat, buy one or borrow one. One group of young men, twelve in number, decided to be pirates. They were able to outfit a thirty-foot boat and sailed down river toward the Bay stopping at any isolated farmhouse that could be seen from the water. They looted the homes, stealing anything of value. Those were the days before many roads bisected the coastal area along Delaware Bay. Many farm's only link with the outside world was by boat. Most of their yearly supplies came to their wharves and they shipped produce and other farm products by boat. Delaware's rivers and streams were the highways in their time.

Usually, the homeowners and their families fled at first sight of the boats filled with young men rowing up the stream toward their wharf. So many stories had been told of vicious pirates that people were cautious when boats loaded with men approached their wharf. When this happened, the entire house was looted. Pigs, chickens, eggs and cured meat were taken to eat and sell after each cruise. On several occasions pirates harassed and looted the isolated farms along the coast of Delaware Bay.

Many of the pirates became over complacent and that led to disaster for them. One day a boatload of pirates approached a wharf located down from a large farmhouse. Seeing no one around, they expected easy pickings. To their surprise on approaching the dock, several men stood up from the reeds and ordered the young pirates to come ashore with hands raised. This command took them by surprise. A number of the lads had muskets and a few flint- lock pistols. They were always bragging about how well armed they were and what they would do should someone resist their efforts as pirates.

One of the pirates raised his musket and aimed at the armed men. He thought that he could intimidate the armed farmers. Instead of the farmers turning and retreating, the five men fired a blast of lead balls at the pirates. Three of the pirates were slightly wounded and the boat suffered damage from being penetrated by lead balls. While the farmers were reloading, the young men manned their oars and fled the scene. They had never been so scared. No one had before offered resistance. While they rowed frantically back toward Delaware Bay they attended their minor wounds. They never thought that being a pirate could be so painful. Each was silently contemplating the fact that being a pirate could be a dangerous occupation. For them, harsh reality took away the excitement of being a pirate.

When the boatload of pirates exited the mouth of the river, they set sail and moved up the Bay. Suddenly one of the pirates yelled, "Look, a sail!" Looking out into the Bay they spied a Navy Ship. It was an armed schooner, flying the Union Jack (English) and it was moving nearer with billowing sails. They knew that outrunning the schooner in their small craft was impossible.

The helmsman steered for shallower water hoping to discourage the schooner, perhaps hoping the schooner would run aground and give up the chase. That didn't happen, and as it gained on them they could see a cannon being run out in preparation for firing.

Suddenly they spied a puff of white smoke followed by a loud "boom" and a whistling sound fast approaching them. The small cannon ball splintered the boat almost in half and it immediately filled with water. Three of the twelve were not swimmers and clung to pieces of the boat. The rest of the pirates swam to the near shore and crawled into the reeds and brush growing profusely along the shore. Utter panic filled the young pirates and they ran inland across the salt meadows in an effort to get as far from the shore as possible.

Four days later the men walked into New Castle. The young men were dirty and their once fine clothing was stained and torn. They had hidden in an abandoned barn hoping the incident would cool down. They entered the Colonial Tavern and ordered food and drink. While they sat enjoying the best meal they had eaten in days, several sailors entered and gathered around a table, ordered food and drink, and started talking about the three pirates they had captured several days before. One asked, "Are you going to the hanging? They are to be hung just before dark this afternoon." Several farmers identified the men as the ones who raided their farms. "They are a bunch of young men. Too bad they are to hang, but the law is the law."

The listening pirates became ashen. What if their buddies betrayed them and they would be rounded up and also hung.

The hanging went as planned by the authorities. Two of the three pirates were begging and pleading for their lives. One was defiant to the end and told his two fellow pirates to be quiet and meet their maker as great pirates would have done.

The young men watched their pirate companions swing at the gallows. That was a lesson hard learned. None of the young men ever returned to piracy and were content to earn their livelihood the hard way.

Chapter 7

Just Meandering

The Heavy Crab Pot

The crabber checked a crab pot set out in the Simmon's River one morning. He was pulling the two non-commercial crab pots by hand. Pulling crab pots by hand is a laborious task and now days most crabbers won't work the water without a motorized pulley that the rope can be wrapped around to pull the crab pot out of the water onto the boat. At one time everyone pulled crab pots by hand. The late waterman "Dicky" Short is reputed to be the first waterman working Delaware Bay to use a motorized pulley for pulling crab pots.

The man grabbed the crab floats and started pulling on the line. Though he exerted all his strength, he couldn't pull the crab pot out of the water. Finally, he attached the line to the boat and started moving forward. To his chagrin his crab pot line had caught on a jet fighter pilot's ejection seat. The seat came to the surface and there he observed a pilot's helmet and what looked like a body attached. He quickly dropped the crab line back into the water and traveled to Port

Mahon where he called the State Police. The police in turn contacted Dover Air Force Base. Soon the area was teeming with Marine Police, State Police, Little Creek's Fire Department and Air Force personnel.

The jet had crashed into the Bay on take- off and the authorities hadn't been able to locate the pilot. Apparently, the pilot had ejected from too low an altitude and his parachute had failed to completely open. We should have nothing but respect for those giving their lives serving our country.

Fish Netting

In the early spring before the water warms many watermen set gill nets for Shad, Weakfish, Flounder and Stripped Bass. At one time the waterman could expect nice catches of the fore-mentioned fish. The work was cold, hard and messy. Most didn't mind because netting fish provided a good income for that time of the year before crabs started running. Most people setting out nets would check their nets daily and remove the catch. The water was still cold enough to prevent the fish spoiling and being unfit for the market. Fresh caught fish would have a healthy red coloring in their gills indicating a recent catch. When the water started to warm, the net fishermen pulled their nets and ended the season. Some would then resort to drift nets that they would set out and stay in the vicinity and occasionally remove fish from the nets. The fish would be placed in a cooler to prevent spoiling.

Sports fishermen and commercial watermen often

resented each other. The sports fishermen thought that the watermen were taking too many fish and that would lead to a shortage of fish in the Bay for them to catch.

The net fishermen resented the recreational fishermen because the fishermen would often damage their nets. There was only a short span of time when both net and sport fishermen would be active. As soon as the water became warm the set nets would be pulled.

The author was crabbing one spring up the Bay from Port Mahon. The crabbing was good. He was pulling the crab pots by hand, all sixty-six of them. It was a tiring, wet, dirty and sometimes, seasick occupation. After all the crab pots had been pulled, he anchored to sort his catch and to clean the mud and slime from the boat.

He had forgotten to bring water or food with him when he had left home at daylight to check his crab pots. It was about noon and the day was hot and sticky. He became very thirsty and hungry. He was muttering under his breath about how stupid he had been in not bringing either food or water with him.

When he pulled his anchor there was a large cluster of oysters caught on one of the anchor points. He started to toss the cluster back overboard when he noticed three unopened oyster shells. (The shells normally open once the oyster dies.) He had never eaten raw oysters before, but he was about starved. He pried open one of the oysters and looked at the blob of oyster and cut it loose and swallowed it. The oyster had a salty taste and wasn't too bad. He soon opened the remaining two oysters and ate them too. That was the first time he had eaten raw oysters and the last time, too. His stomach did feel better after eating the raw oysters. Hungry as he was, he guessed anything would have tasted good.

He got underway and traveled down the Bay toward the entrance to Little River. His boat dock was two miles up Little River in the village of Little Creek.

On the way, he spied a boat checking a stationary fish net. He wondered who would have a net out so late in the season. The water was so warm that fish would spoil when caught in the net for any length of time.

When he approached the man checking the net, he recognized a local character who lived in Little Creek. The man was a well-liked character who hung out around Little Creek doing odd jobs. He did some net fishing and trapped a few muskrats in the winter to supplement his small social security check. Often he would sleep in an old disabled van and for a time slept in the Laughing Gull, a small tavern in Little Creek, to prevent anyone from breaking in. He was honest, an eccentric individual and some might think of him as a never-do-well sort of person. Everybody in the little village seemed to like him.

He motored up to where the man was checking his net. In the conversation that followed the man checking his net discovered that he was thirsty and offered him a beer. The problem was that he didn't drink, and didn't like beer. He asked the man if he had water.

"No" was the answer, "I don't drink that stuff. Here drink this beer, it's cold and it will do you good."

Reluctantly he accepted the bottle of cold beer. Nothing had ever tasted better!

After finishing the bottle of beer and refusing another beer, he asked the man why he hadn't taken up his net since the season for net fishing was over?

"I just ain't got around to it," the man replied. "Besides, I'm still catching fish. Whenever I need beer money, I come out and take recently caught fish into Little Creek and sell them at Marvel's fish market."

Looking at the net revealed it filled with fish in various stages of decay. The filled net must have held tons of fish. Some were thirty to forty inch Weakfish. The sharks were having a feeding frenzy with all the trapped fish. The water was boiling with their activities.

"Don't you think you might get in trouble with Eager Thompson (He operated the State Boat and worked for the Division of Fish and Wildlife). I bet the local fishermen will be very angry if they should see all of these fish rotting in your net."

The man admitted that was a problem and knew he had better take the net up. Rather than waiting to be asked to help take up the net, he thanked the man for the beer and sped off to his dock in Little Creek where he could get some water to drink. He was dry!

Of all the characters the author had met in his lifetime, the eccentric man from Little Creek, who lived in an old van, would rank at the top of the list. He died a few years later, alone in an old van.

The Novice Crabber

In 1968, the author purchased an old boat and would launch it at the Port Mahon docks. Traveling on such a large body of water was exciting to say the least. A fellow teacher wanted to accompany him whenever the boat was launched. A 1955 Mercury 70 HP motor powered the boat. The only problem with the Silver Streak motor was that it had to be turned off before placing the gear in reverse. After shifting into reverse, the motor had to be restarted. Sometimes this situation caused problems. Once the boat was approaching the Port Mahon docks when the motor was cut off and the gear placed in reverse. The only problem was that the motor wouldn't start and the boat slammed into a corner of the boat ramp. The impact knocked a five- inch hole in the forward side of the boat. The hole was above the water line and easy to later patch.

It is said that people learn from experience. That was sure the situation involving the author and his friend and their first experience on Delaware Bay. It seems like yesterday when they launched the 18-foot wooden boat and accelerated down the Mahon River for the Bay. The words "Slow, No Wake" had no meaning at that time.

That first trip almost ended in disaster as the boat sped down the river. The man traveling with the author decided to walk on a small ledge around the cabin so he could sit on the bow of the boat. About half way toward the bow his feet slipped on the wet ledge and he fell overboard. The boat was moving at about thirty MPH and leaving a large wake.

Immediately the boat operator slowed the boat and turned back to attempt locating his friend. His friend had a head of hair that some of his balding friends envied. His hair was black and gave him a very handsome look. The man could be seen about one hundred yards upstream where he had fallen overboard. The driver slowly eased to where the man was treading water and couldn't believe what he saw. The man was bald except around the edges of his scalp. His hair was long and he had used the long hair to make a comb-over that gave him the appearance of having beautiful hair. He fished his cap out of the water and covered his wet hair so his bald head wouldn't show.

The author and his friend decided to get into the crabbing business and work after school each day and on Saturdays. In the summer they could work all day.

The man taught Shop in school. He said that he would have his students build crab pots for them. He asked the dimensions of a crab pot and the author told him that he thought a crab pot would be about 24" X 24".

After a week the students in the shop classes had made ten crab pots as a school project for which they were paid a small sum. The "would be" crabbers picked up the pots and soon arrived at Port Mahon with the extra large crab pots. To their dismay, there was a large number of crab pots stacked near the docks. Those pots were really much smaller than the pots they had had made. The men thought, "What difference does the size of a crab pot make?" They soon found out!

No one else had crab pots in the water at that time. The two men baited their crab pots with chicken necks and a short distance from the mouth of the Mahon River, they started dropping pots overboard. White plastic bleach bottles were used for floats. They were ignorant of how to place their pots. Instead of setting them up and down the Bay, they made a straight line out into the Bay. That arrangement probably caused a few of the old timers to chuckle.

They had set out the crab pots on a Friday afternoon and could hardly sleep that night in anticipation of checking the crab pots the next morning.

By eight AM, they had launched the boat and were checking the first crab pot. There was no problem locating the crab pots. The water was smooth like a tabletop. The first pot pulled out of the water proved to be a difficult task requiring both of our efforts. The pot was filled with crabs. Each of the following pots was filled. Out of ten crab pots they had four baskets of crabs. We couldn't believe our good fortune. Wow! Just think, catching crabs in that volume would earn lots of dollars.

Later in the day we sold the crabs to William's seafood business in Little Heaven. When we returned to the dock with our crabs, a Ford pick- up was parked there. The man driving the truck asked a few questions, shook his head and then drove off.

Monday afternoon after school we hurried to the Mahon boat ramp. Looking from the road on the way to the docks we could hardly believe the large number of floats marking crab pots in the water off Port

Mahon.

Approaching our crab pots was very difficult because there was line after line of floats as far as we could see running up and down the Bay. They then realized that they were really novices at the art of crabbing. The crab pots only held two baskets of crabs on the second day of crabbing.

Pulling the heavy pots was too much of an effort each day, so we pulled all the pots and later the author talked to an experienced man who had worked years on the water about crabbing. The man (Herman Moore) explained all about crabbing and how it was done. He sold the author 50 crab pots, zincs, rope, iron rods for weights and 150 cork floats.

That transaction started an interesting five years working on the water. The author went through several partners, all quickly grew tired of being sea sick, dirty and wet. Many were afraid of being pinched by the crabs. One man even invested money and after three trips told the author that he could keep the money, but he would never go out on the water again. He couldn't get accustomed to being sea sick and getting dirty when pulling in the crab pots by hand. He was fine on the water until he would start pulling a pot and looking down at the water. That made him very sick and he would start vomiting.

After the first year crabbing, the author truly became the "Lone Crabber" which was his CB Radio's call sign. He purchased a new 22' open, center console, fiber-glass boat powered by a 70 HP motor. He worked alone on the Bay about five years and docked his boat at a rented slip in Little Creek. The first spring that he placed his 100- yard gill net in the water south of the entrance to Little River was very exciting.

Excitedly, he approached his gill net shortly after daylight and couldn't believe the tremendous catch in the net.

The net was filled with weakfish and menhaden (bunkers) and a few Rays. Taking the fish from the net by pulling it over the boat was time consuming. There was debris caught in the net and Rays tangled in it in several places.

He already had a market for fish fillets for fellow teachers and neighbors. His freezer was full of the bounty from the Bay. The small store in Little Creek took orders for the crabs and fish that he caught. A seafood place across from the Base's main gate (Salty Sarge) also purchased a portion of his catch. He didn't make a large amount of money, but the venture supported his love of outdoor activities such as fishing and boating.

The years rapidly passed. He enjoyed working on the water and learned much about his own ability and others as well. When on the water a person is his own boss and most people on the water love the outdoors. The Bay grows on a person. He thought, "Why should I take a vacation. I have it all right here on the Bay." He had to admit that his wife had other ideas about where to go on vacation.

Once a person has worked on the water it is easy to understand why people like that activity. It gives one a sense of independence and being in control, that is until a storm catches a person unaware and then he realizes how little and powerless man is compared to the might of a storm roaring down the Bay.

The author decided that he would become a full time waterman and enrolled in a class to acquire his Captain's License. He wanted to legally take small parties fishing. By that time he had learned a lot about working on the water. There is always the unexpected happening on the water. He experienced several situations that could have proven disastrous to the unwary.

All good things must come to an end. He had once lived in the Arctic for several years and the cold had affected his joints. He started having trouble with his right ankle. (It later was fused together twice) and then both shoulders and knees had to be replaced. These health conditions killed all aspirations to work on the water.

Selling his boat was a difficult thing to do. But, the boat and crab pots would only deteriorate sitting in his yard. Reluctantly he sold his equipment. Every time he would see his old boat, wonderful memories of the wind blowing in his face and the rocking of the boat while working on the Bay surged through his mind. As people grow older such memories are indeed cherished.

Bad Luck Crabber

Sometimes, no matter how hard one tries, nothing seems to go right. Such was the case of a once well - known Waterman who worked out of Port Mahon near

Little Creek. This man worked several years crabbing and netting fish. One of the first stories the author heard about this man's bad luck was about the time he was in Simmon's River North of Port Mahon. He had a few crab pots set in the river. The boat was idling when he tossed overboard a crab pot that he had just emptied and re-baited. His glove got caught on a piece of wire on the trap and since he was off balance, he went overboard with the crab pot. He pulled loose from the crab pot and found himself in shallow water and stuck in the mud. His helper was new, having never worked on the Bay before.

The crabber yelled for the helper to toss him a rope and move the boat forward and pull him from the mud. The man attached a rope to a cleat on the boat, made a lasso and tossed it toward the stranded crabber. Unfortunately, the rope made a perfect landing around his neck. Before he could open the noose wider to position it under his arm pits, the helper accelerated the boat and started dragging him through the water. Luckily for him, he was able to grasp the rope and hold on for dear life. He was dragged about one hundred feet through the water. He was almost in terror with the thought that he couldn't hold onto the rope much longer and would be strangled if he let go.

To his relief, the helper stopped the boat.

The crabber yelled unprintable words at the helper and told him to throw the anchor on to the riverbank and pull the boat against the bank and help him from the water. Now this man was a huge person and it wasn't a little task to help him onto the bank and back into the boat. He had once been a pro wrestler and was a big man. His nickname was "Fat Daddy."

After a tremendous struggle, the man crawled through the mud and water and up the bank. He was soaking wet and covered with mud. He was fortunate to have had a helper along. Should he have been alone, the incident could have cost him his life.

Another time the "black cloud of woe" that seemed to follow him witnessed him falling from the dock at Jenkins Wharf. Jenkins Wharf once was located where the public boat ramp at Port Mahon is now situated. Harry "Pretty" Killen started operating the wharf in the 1940s. "Fat Daddy" fell from the dock and landed on a steel bolt protruding up that once held part of the dock together. He fell from the wharf—it wasn't clear what caused him to fall—and was impaled on the sharp point of the bolt. This was a serious incident and could have been fatal. His screams alerted crabbers who were at the wharf or inside the small café located there. It required local watermen who happened to be in the area to pull him from the piling.

Two of the watermen took him to Kent General Hospital for treatment. He was very fortunate! The sharp-pointed bolt that penetrated his body punctured no vital organ. Sitting down was an ordeal for a couple of weeks. He has been dead several years now, but fondly remembered by those who worked on the water with him.

That Tide Runs Fast

Sometimes, on a hot humid day, people fishing on the Bay decide to take a swim. Most watermen wouldn't consider swimming in the Bay except during emergencies. Many have seen the huge and numerous sharks found in the Bay and want nothing to do with these creatures other than catching them on a line and cutting them into steaks for the freezer. However, on occasions, the naive do attempt swimming and water skiing. The Bay is a poor place to ski because often the water is too rough for skiing. Sometimes people do it anyway.

Sometimes when the tide is running people have been known to attempt swimming from one anchored boat to another. In most situations that is an impossible task. The same situation exists when the tide is running and someone falls overboard from their boat---that has actually happened a number of times, and they discover that the boat drifts with the outgoing tide faster than they can swim. That happened to Mr. Graves who lives in Harbeson, DE a few years ago. He ended up treading water till after 12:30AM before he was rescued.

One Waterman, Wayne "Big Daddy" Mills, told the author that once his son failed to heed his advice and attempted to swim about one hundred feet to another anchored boat that contained some of his friends. He dove overboard and started swimming. The tide carried him swiftly away from the boat. The waterman wanted to teach his son a lesson, so he decided not to up anchor and pick him up at that moment. Instead, he tossed two life preservers toward his son who was able to grasp both preservers. The father let his son drift with the tide for several hundred yards before he pulled anchor and picked him up. That lesson about bucking the tide stayed with the son who is now much older and much wiser.

The same young man, like many young men working the water, was quite a prankster. Once he was helping his father and a crewman check crab pots. The young man kept splashing water on the crewman and pretended to attempt throwing the man overboard.

The man was of slight build and after a time grew tired of the teasing and told the young man to stop the teasing. The teasing was really affecting the man's work. After all, no one in their right mind enjoyed the thought of being tossed overboard. The father also told the young man to stop the teasing, but the son didn't listen and continued what he was doing. Finally, the father grew tired of his son's antics, and once when his son pretended he was going to throw the crewman overboard, he reached over and grasped the young man by his belt and collar and tossed him overboard.

The kid came to the surface spitting water and the father wouldn't take him back aboard the boat until he promised to stop the kidding and pranks. He quickly promised and only then did his father pull him back aboard the boat. The young man kept his word because he knew that his father was as good as his word and wouldn't hesitate to toss him back overboard. His was a well-learned lesson.

Wayne Mills, Sr. reflects on the "good old days" when he caught 12,000 peeler crabs in one day.

This waterman's (Wayne "Big Daddy" Mills) proudest day was when he caught over 12,000 peeler crabs (Crabs that are in the process of shedding their shells). Crabs in the process of shedding make good fish bait and are sold for processing into soft-shell crabs that are an Eastern Shore delicacy. That was perhaps a record catch for one crabber in a day. Peelers were selling for forty cents each to crab buyers.

Captain Wayne "Big Daddy" Mills worked on the Bay for many years and now because of health problems and disappointment from a number of bad years on the Bay, he has retired as a waterman. If crabs once again became plentiful and decent help to man his boat could be found, I'm sure he would be back working on the water. He remembers working for Herman Moore when he was a young man and all the things he learned from that outstanding waterman. Captain Moore was one of many people who in the 1940s chose to earn a living from Delaware Bay. He left a factory job and never regretted his decision.

Though Wayne Mills isn't working on the water, his heart is still there. The old quote "Once a waterman, always a waterman" holds true for many people who still yearn for the freedom of working on Delaware Bay.

The Dolphin

In the spring 2006, a crabber, Joey Smith, out of Flemmings Landing, was working a long line of crab pots out in the Bay north of Port Mahon. An unusual incident occurred. While he was baiting a crab pot, he was startled to see the upper portion of a large fish lunge out of the water. It was a large Dolphin. There are Dolphins in the Bay that are often seen by watermen from a distance, but never had one surfaced next to a boat.

This Dolphin was begging for food. The waterman tossed several bait fish (bunkers) and the Dolphin caught the small fish in the air. It kept begging and swimming around the boat. The waterman wasn't about to feed the Dolphin a large portion of his bait-fish. After the Dolphin realized the waterman wasn't going to give more food, it swam to where other waterman were working their crab pots and begged food from several of them.

Dolphin

The Department of Fish and Wildlife was contacted. After some research, they discovered that a Dolphin had been tagged 37 years before and held in captivity in Florida. The Dolphin had been tagged with an identifying number on its fin before release. The Dolphin had been sighted previously on several occasions all the way from Florida to New Jersey. I guess the term, "Once a beggar, always a beggar," applied to this beautiful and intelligent creature from the sea. A waterman experiencing a creature suddenly poking its head out of the water begging food can be startling and very exciting.

Jack Pleasanton's boat Miss Ruth (Named after his wife) with load of oysters

Jack Pleasanton's boat Janice at Port Mahon, Delaware dock

Jeanette Killen standing on her dock in Leipsic, Delaware
Note the number 1 sign on the crabbing boat. Her husband Harry "Pretty" Killen was issued the first shell fish license.

Frenchie's Dock at Bowers Beach

Beautiful swimmers (Rock Fish) from Delaware Bay.

Captain Sonny Burrows Leipsic, Delaware
Sonny has worked as a waterman on Delaware Bay for about 50 years.

Little Creek Market, built in the early 1950s presently serves as a market and deli. The food is good and the employees friendly. Many watermen, bird watchers and hunters have eaten there.

Smithy's bait and tackle shop in Leipsic, Delaware is a good place to buy bait and tackle.

Captain Jack Deadeye Pleasanton worked many years on Delaware Bay as an oysterman and a crabber.

Captain Craig Pugh with crew dredge for oysters

The old *Maggie Myers*, perhaps the oldest boat working on Delaware Bay (Keel laid in 1897) was rigged by her owner, Frank "Thumper" Eicherly to dredge oysters and crabs with sail power.

Wayne Herbie Mills hopes he will have a profitable season crabbing on Delaware Bay. He is a second generation crabber.

Chapter 8

Beware How You Anchor

Delaware Bay is a dangerous body of water for the unaware and novice boater. Some out-of-state fishermen arrive at one of the numerous boat ramps and launch their boats with the intention of spending the day fishing and moving around the Bay to different locations in an effort to catch fish. Many fishermen are rewarded by good catches of Weakfish, Blues, Stripes, Black Bass and Flounder. Of course fishing isn't nearly as good as it was twenty years ago, and perhaps never will get better.

Being on the Bay is very exciting to a person who has never before boated on a large body of water, or boated infrequently. There are many major pitfalls for those not acclimated to the Bay. The first problem is the weather. Those who work on the water are very conscience of weather conditions. Many watermen see dark clouds coming down the Bay and they will head in to the safety of a river or dock area. One waterman spotted a waterspout heading down the Bay toward his boat. He was able to move out of the way of the approaching waterspout. That was a scary situation.

During crabbing season certain areas of the Bay are filled with floats marking the thousands of crab pots set in the Bay. It is easy to cut floats loose by accidentally passing over the rope attached to the floats and crab pots. Sometimes a propeller gets wrapped with a rope when a boater runs over it and then the rope has to be cut off. Often the boats have to be towed into the launching ramp and pulled out of the water to remove the rope tangled in the propeller.

Some recreational fishermen who experience this situation often blame the crabber for having the rope where it can be run over. Of course, the waterman isn't to blame. He's just earning his living crabbing. Low tide is when it is easier to run over crab pot lines.

If a boater thinks he has problems from running over and cutting a rope, how do you think crabbers feel from having some careless boater running over and cutting their floats? After all, when a line is cut the crabber loses a crab pot usually valued at over forty dollars. This makes for some hard feelings. Most fishermen are careful not to run over crab pot lines.

After a time, the men working the Bay become callous from witnessing unbelievable acts of plain stupidity from some of the many boaters fishing in the Bay. Most are very seasoned fishermen and watch out for crab floats, but there is always a small number that act out of ignorance, stupidity or just plain carelessness.

One type of trouble fishermen who are new to the Bay gets into is incorrectly anchoring their boats. For some reason they think the cleats on the sides of boats are for anchoring while they are fishing. Many toss anchors overboard and tie the rope to the rear of the boat.

If the water is calm and the tide not moving fast, that's okay. However, when the tide changes or the wind gets up like it often does on the Bay, the fishermen are in deep trouble. On most inland rivers, creeks and small lakes it makes little difference how you anchor.

On the Bay, how a boat is anchored can become a serious problem. In 1975, two men from Pennsylvania learned the hard way that anchoring from the stern is dangerous. The two were new to the Bay and were about a mile out and slightly north of the entrance to the St. Jones River. They had good fortune fishing and when the tide turned, the wind increased and the waves were suddenly running 3'-4'. The stern was pulled under and the men found themselves in the water. The men didn't have time to even put on their life preservers. The boat had floatation built in, but the boat was too unstable to get back into. All they could do was cling to their boat in the cold rough water. After several hours of enduring the cold water they begin to tire and started having a difficult time holding onto the boat. When they were almost ready to give up, a passing waterman spotted them and took them aboard his boat and towed the water-filled boat back into Bowers Beach. The men were very fortunate to have been rescued. Theirs was a lesson learned the hard way.

Over the years many watermen have witnessed such incidents and some decided to teach fishermen a lesson when they were spotted anchored from the stern. If old people or small children were aboard, they would issue a warning. Many fishermen so warned are embarrassed and sometimes tell the watermen to mind their own business, and they do! It's often open season on adults who are seen anchored from the stern. If a wave fills the fishermen's boat and it sinks, most won't stop and rescue the victims. Instead, they call the Marine Police and fire station rescue people. If the victims are in serious trouble, most would pull the fishermen from the water. They seem to enjoy watching the boaters as they learn a lesson the hard way. Perhaps many people need to learn things the hard way so they will remember. The sad aspect to fishing on the Bay is that it can be unforgiving.

Sometimes well-meaning boaters run into problems that they couldn't anticipate ever happening to them. One waterman tells of an incident at Bowers Beach where a beautiful yacht, operated by an apparently inexperienced person ran aground while turning in the Murderkill River. The waterman attached a line to the yacht and pulled it free. The yacht operator said he was running out of fuel and wanted to know where he could refuel. No facility was available at Bowers for the man to refuel his boat.

The waterman carried an extra five gallons of gas on his boat for emergencies. The waterman told the boat operator to tie up at the public dock area and he would sell him the extra five gallons of gas that was on his boat. The operator steered his boat to the dock and when the waterman grabbed a line and tied the yacht to the dock, the yacht operator reversed his motor and broke off the 4 x 4 post to which the waterman had just tied the yacht. After much maneuvering the yacht was secured to the dock.

The waterman didn't know how far the yacht could travel on five gallons of gas. The last he saw of the yacht it was heading down the channel toward the open Bay. There is knowledge on operating large boats that can only be gained from experience. Some people think that all one has to do is climb aboard a boat and everything will work out fine. All it takes to educate a boat operator is to be caught is a storm on Delaware Bay. Then, a person comes to the realization of how little they really know about boating.

Chapter 9

The Trap Line

People who trap muskrats during the cold winter months are a hardy breed of men. Think of being in the marsh by daylight wading ditches and often through deep mud checking each trap to see what it holds. Many people have for generations, operated trap lines. Once it was the only thing that kept families in the coastal areas surviving economically. Conditions are constantly changing because of the fashion cycle that dictates whether long hair or short hair furs will be in demand. The trapper is a victim to fashions. Most of the time, the lowly muskrat has been in demand. And then, there are the misguided people who want to make trapping illegal.

Delaware has been blessed with large marshes and an abundance of waterfowl and fur bearing animals. Many watermen and farm families once trapped the marshes. Muskrats and raccoons were caught for their fur as well as flesh. At one time those living near the marshes considered muskrats on par with chicken for eating. The muskrats are prepared several ways for the table. Often the flesh is boiled with onions to take away the wild taste, then baked, fried or stewed.

Many politicians in olden times and some living today host muskrat dinners that are still well attended. One old waterman said that if it hadn't been for the lowly muskrat, he and his family would have starved during the dark days of the Great Depression. The money from the pelts bought coffee, flour, sugar and clothing. The muskrat's flesh could also be made into a spicy sausage.

One older farmer related that before the Great Depression (1929-1942), he would usually plant large fields of corn and raise hundreds of hogs. The problem that beset the nation finally reached out to the farmers and they discovered there was little or no market for hogs, beef cattle or corn. Some farmers, during those difficult times turned their corn into corn whiskey. It seems that some people always have money to buy spirits.

Farm products dropped in demand because no one had money.

Most people in the small towns and rural areas started raising their own cow for milk, chickens for meat and eggs, a hog or two to supply lard for cooking and meat for the table. Combined with a large garden most lived well as far as food was concerned. Those living in large cities really suffered during the Depression.

This particular farmer stopped planting large acreages in corn, wheat or barley and started trapping muskrats in the large marsh adjacent to his farm. Even when farm products were a glut on the market, there was a big demand for muskrat pelts. For several years he trapped his marshes and discovered that he could earn several thousand dollars a year strictly from the lowly muskrat. Not only was there a market for the pelts, but also for the meat. He could sell the meat from the muskrats he trapped for ten to fifteen cents and the muskrat skins for twenty-five to fifty-five cents each. (Some years the pelt brought one dollar). That was a good sum in those days.

Many people at that time were unemployed or under employed. Some, who could find jobs during the Great Depression (1929-1942) earned only five to ten dollars a week. There were always exceptions and some people did have better jobs that paid more. Fortunately, Delaware wasn't hit as hard by the Depression as other areas of the nation.

For several years the farmer earned a good income trapping muskrats while the average person earned several hundred dollars a year, that is, if he had a decent job. Most years the trapper would trap in excess of 10,000 muskrats. Not only did he do well, but also many Delaware trappers were able to earn above average wages trapping.

With the advent of World War II, muskrat trapping became even more profitable because muskrat fur was used to line flight helmets, clothing and gloves. Muskrat fur is warm and durable. That made it in great demand.

Walking a marsh isn't as easy as it looks. The author once invited a friend who was interested in the outdoors and trapping to accompany him on his trap line. The man had never been on a marsh before and the first wrong thing he did was over dress. He wore a heavy coat, mitts, hat and hip boots. He wanted to stay warm. Dressing like that was a big mistake.

Walking some marshes can be difficult because of the deep mud that a person has to travel over. The trick is to step on the grass hassocks—clumps of grass and sod—and not between them. Almost immediately the man stepped off into the mud. He started sinking in the mud and because of his heavy clothing was unable to extract himself. He was soon up to his waist in the mud and unable to move. It was humorous to the trapper, but a panic situation for the man who had never before waded in a marsh. After the trapper stopped laughing, he was able, with great difficulty, to pull the man from the mud.

The trapped man didn't think the incident was humorous at all. Had the man ventured into the marsh alone, he would probably still be there under the mud. Trapping can be dangerous. Needless to say, the man never again entered a Delaware marsh. He stated that "Once to have walked over a Delaware Marsh, and getting trapped in the mud was an experience he would never again attempt." And he didn't! He thought the trapper somewhat deranged to trap such a dangerous area as a marsh, and sometimes in the dark using only a flashlight to find his way. Trappers are a different breed of men. Perhaps they hear drum beats that others don't hear.

Chapter 10

Overnight on a Flooded Marsh

One cold January day a trapper—Bill Cook—drove to the edge of a marsh near Wilmington to check his muskrat traps. He parked his car along side the road and started walking the ditches and marsh area checking traps. The wind had risen to about thirty mph and that made it even colder. He had to wade across three ditches to reach all of his traps that were spread out for three-quarters of a mile across the marsh.

The tide had started to come in and combined with a full moon and strong wind, soon filled all the ditches that he had to wade across to reach the marsh meadow when he trapped. After a time, to his chagrin, water started flooding the marsh. The water was too cold to swim-ice was floating in it, and he was a poor swimmer. He was wearing hip boots and already the water was half up to his knees.

He was concerned about his predicament at first and didn't know what to do. He realized that he needed higher ground, but everything was level with ditches running through the marsh. He decided to make his own high ground. He located an exceptionally large muskrat house and started dragging small piles of reeds and other muskrat houses and placing them on top of the one large house. Soon, he was at the highest location in the marsh. Still, the water kept rising until he was again about knee deep in the icy water. In sum, he spent the entire night standing in the water on top of the pile of reeds and muskrat houses. He stayed there until the wind ebbed and the tide started running out.

During the night his concerned family drove to where his car was parked. They aimed the car's lights across the marsh and flashed them off and on to see if they could locate him. They couldn't see him at first. Once they turned the lights off, they saw a small light flare up in the distance. It was their father and husband lighting a cigarette. The light was a small pinpoint.

Seeing that confirmed that he was still living. They knew he was a hardy soul. They could see the water covered marsh that looked like a large lake, too. They remained by his car until near dawn when he came wading back toward his car through the receding tide. His only compliant was that he had run out of cigarettes.

"Cookie" as he was called, was able to acquire a contract from the government, at an above average price, to supply a certain number of muskrat pelts to a Government Purchasing Agent. That winter, he earned 4,800.00 dollars. The homes in his area didn't have indoor plumbing, so he used the money earned from trapping to install the first indoor bathroom in his community.

Many "Old-timers" still remember Bill Cook, or

"Cookie" as he was known. He possessed an above average love for outdoor activities. Wherever the older watermen gather his name occasionally comes up.

NOTE: Bill Cook's last day on earth was doing what he enjoyed most, ... duck hunting. The day he died was opening day for duck season. He went hunting at dawn and soon shot his limit of ducks. He took them home, ate a quick breakfast and then rushed back to his duck blind to shoot another limit of ducks. On the way home he died when his car left the road and struck a tree. A medical examination showed that he had a massive heart attack and was already dead when his car left the road. He had always said that when his time came he hoped he would be hunting. He got his last wish.

Many interesting stories come from those who trap the marshes. One is about two young men who lived near a small marsh that appeared to have a large muskrat population evident by the many muskrat houses scattered across the marsh. The marsh belonged to a family living in Florida.

Many people would have liked to trap that small marsh, but decided not to trap there without permission and maybe get into trouble. A few had written the family who owned the land and had never received an answer to their request. Two young men decided that they would trap that marsh even though they had no permission.

One cold day in December they dressed in hip waders and each carrying a bundle of poles with traps attached walked the short distance to the edge of the marsh. When they started wading into the marsh, a man who lived near, rushed out of his house and asked them if they had permission to trap the marsh. They replied that they didn't and the owners living in Florida probably didn't care either.

The man attempted to discourage them—most likely he had been thinking about trapping the marsh and had waited too late. Seeing he couldn't discourage the young men, he told them that since he lived near the marsh, he had probably more right than they did to trap there. Since they were determined to trap the marsh, he told them that he wouldn't say anything if they would supply him with fresh muskrats to eat during the time they were trapping. The boys agreed!

The first night they had a good catch and from one of the traps near shore they found a large tomcat that had been caught in a trap and drowned. When they skinned their catch they included the cat.

The man had told them that he loved muskrats and for them to stop by on the way home each day and give him a muskrat. They took their skinned muskrat carcasses by the man's house and he laid them on the table and selected the biggest carcass, which was the cat. One of the boys asked him if he was sure he wanted the biggest of the muskrat carcasses. He replied to the affirmative and took the large cat carcass and one of the largest of the muskrats. The boys could hardly contain themselves as the man thanked them and told them to stop by a few times each week and give him more muskrats.

The next day when they came to the man's house

where the path led to the marsh, he stopped them. He told them that the bigger of the two muskrats they had given him, (he had demanded them), was the best tasting muskrat that he could remember from many years of eating muskrats. They told him that they would definitely save him any other "large muskrats" that they might catch.

Once they entered the marsh and were out of sight of the man, they could hardly control themselves. They laughed so hard that it brought tears to their eyes. They hoped to catch another large cat or maybe a skunk to give him, but that never happened. They had a good year trapping before the owners finally sold the marsh to a local man.

Chapter 11

Alcohol and Boating

Many people boating on the Bay during summer fill their coolers with several six packs of beer so that they can have "a cold one" during the heat of the day. Drinking too much beer can be devastating by impairing the boater's reaction time. During emergencies a cool head is very important.

Several men who work on the water often motor into the Bay with beer to drink during the heat of the day. Most only drink a few cans of beer during the course of a day working on the water. When a large number of fishermen are in the Bay it is common to see beer cans floating on the water with the tide.

A deck hand on one of the crab boats several years ago would leave the boat at the end of the day staggering. No one could figure out how he got drunk since he didn't drink beer and there was no evidence of him having a bottle. He claimed to have a bad stomach and had to eat baby food because of his medical problem. He would always bring aboard the boat ten or twelve baby food jars and during the course of the day he would stop and consume a jar of "food." Everyone felt sorry for the man having such a delicate stomach.

One day while he was sorting crabs, the boat captain took one of the "baby food jars" and opened it. It was filled with a clear liquid, maybe gin. The contents didn't have an alcohol smell. The man quickly emptied the jars into the Bay and refilled each with Bay water.

Throughout the rest of the day the helper would "eat" some of the baby food. The man drank at least six of the baby food jars filled with Bay water and apparently couldn't tell the difference between gin and Bay water. As far as the other men knew the man suffered no ill effects from drinking the Bay water. That was one day that he didn't leave the boat staggering.

One day while coming up the Leipsic River, we saw a man tied up to the shore in a small boat. He wasn't fishing, but sitting in the boat. He waved our boat over and we stopped to see what he wanted. His first words uttered were, "You're stealing from my crab pots." That utterance was followed by a stream of profanity. That came as a shock because of two things, first, we had only seen the man once before, and second, we definitely weren't stealing from anyone's crab pots. And we didn't appreciate being cursed at. Immediately we discerned that he was very intoxicated.

What were they to do about the situation? Then, to make matters worse, he stood up in the boat and attempted to strike one of the men in our party. He missed and fell over backwards into the bottom of his boat. The boat contained two to three inches of filthy water consisting of a mixture of fish scales, blood and rotten fish bait. Almost immediately he went into a deep sleep and started snoring.

We weren't worried too much about the man because other boats would be coming in later in the afternoon. We left the man snoring in the bottom of his boat surrounded by Green Head Flies. The man was well known in Leipsic and Little Creek and would occasionally "hit the bottle" to excess. He survived the ordeal and couldn't seem to remember anything about the incident.

Chapter 12

Sturgeon Fishing

Sturgeons are a throwback to primitive times and were once the most sought after fish in the Delaware River and Bay. Sturgeons spawn in streams leading into Delaware Bay and were once caught in great numbers using nets. The eggs of the Sturgeon are used for caviar, the flesh has a consistency similar to tuna and at one time the protective bony plate covering the top and sides of the fish was used as material for buttons. There was a small button manufacturing company in New Jersey during the early Twentieth Century. That company served as a market for the bony armor from the sturgeons. There are two species of the Sturgeon in the Bay: Long nose and short nose. This fish can grow to a length of 14 -20 feet.

A large Sturgeon is capable of producing many pounds of roe that was once sold to buyers from Russia. Russia was the largest caviar producer in the World, especially back in Imperial Russia before the Communist came to power in 1917. During the spawning season nets were placed in the mouths of small streams and out in the Delaware River off both Delaware and New Jersey shores.

The Interpretative Center in Port Penn has this outstanding display of a Sturgeon and the prehistoric bony plate that covered most of the Sturgeon's body.

Sturgeons are bottom feeders and the watermen would place the bottom of the net so it contacted the stream bottom. The larger fish were difficult to handle because of their size. A Sturgeon fisherman was a special breed of man who developed skills from trial and error. Lucky was the young man whose family had been in the Sturgeon fishing business for many years. Under that situation, he grew up in the business and was taught by his father. Today there are still several older men who once were master Sturgeon fishermen. Many live in the Port Penn and Delaware City area.

Pollution and over fishing greatly reduced the Sturgeon fishing industry. At one time Sturgeons were protected in an effort to allow the numbers to increase.

Even today, net fishermen sometimes capture a Sturgeon in their nets during the spring fishing season. Most are caught by accident and are dressed and placed in freezers for later consumption. None caught seem to be as large as those captured in bygone years.

Chapter 13

The Outdoorsman

In parts of Delaware along Route 9, several farmers have hunting clubs. They allow their customers to hunt geese, ducks, deer, quail and pheasants. All are beset by a problem; red fox abound in the area and deplete wild game such as rabbit, quail and pheasant. The farm owners stock the hunting clubs with domestically raised quail and pheasant that seems ever easier for fox to catch.

The end of a successful day of Brant hunting at Indian River Bay in Southern Delaware

Left-Right: Craig Pugh, Horace Pugh and George Shreppler

Horace Pugh setting out decoys

Red fox can't be trapped for their fur in Delaware as they once were. However, special permits can be obtained to trap the excess fox and raccoon. It is unbelievable the amount of prey that is required to feed a vixen and her brood of pups. One man reported seeing the remains of ten muskrat carcasses outside of one fox den. Since red fox have been protected, their numbers have increased to an unbelievable number.

If predators aren't controlled in a hunting area, the area can be fast depleted of small game. The predators have few natural enemies and because of this, they reproduce at an amazing rate. Red fox living near the marshes can wipe out hundreds of muskrats a year to feed their pups. Quail and pheasants that are released for hunting and aren't killed by hunters don't survive more than a month or two because of fox and raccoon.

Craig Pugh returning from a successful day crabbing

A few people still earn their living entirely from working on the water in the summer, trapping and guiding hunters in the winter months. One such person is Craig Pugh of Leipsic, Delaware. He is good at what he does and loves his job. He is often called on by owners of hunting clubs to thin out predators such as fox and raccoon. He has established a reputation of being an exceptionally good waterman, guide and trapper.

Craig with a raccoon he had just caught.

A red fox caught in trap.

Craig with dredge filled with oysters

Chapter 14

The Indian River Life Saving Station

People traveling from Dewey Beach to Bethany Beach can stop and enjoy the seashore along Highway 1. The Department of Parks and Recreation has done a marvelous job creating accesses to the various beach areas. There are swimming areas, fishing areas and access in certain designated areas for four wheel drive vehicles to the beach. A permit is required for taking vehicles onto the beach.

Several years ago a group of teenagers borrowed a dad's four-wheel drive vehicle late one evening, and with several friends, drove onto the beach. Apparently, the driver was a bit too daring and got the vehicle stuck in loose sand. To make a long story short, the vehicle was caught by an incoming tide before the boys could return with help to free the stuck vehicle. The vehicle was a total loss from being submerged in sand and salt water.

When traveling down the highway just before the Indian River Inlet Bridge, on the north bound lane, there is a bit of history maintained by the Division of

Parks and Recreation. It's a restored Life Saving Station. The building has been restored to what it was like in 1905.

Sign located in front of the Indian River Life Saving Station.

After the Civil War, water commerce grew at a rapid rate and to help vessels in distress, Life saving stations were established all along the Atlantic Seaboard. Crews patrolled portions of the beach and maintained a watch for vessels in distress. It was a lonely job. Today it is difficult to imagine what a wild and lonely stretch of beach that area was before a road was built. The station was supplied by boat.

The 1905 Life Saving Station at Indian River

Life boat used for early rescue missions.

Crews from that station participated in several actual rescues. Rescues were accomplished by dragging a heavy wooden boat over the sand dunes to the beach and rowing out through heavy surfs to rescue people in distress from floundering ships. Many ships ran aground on sand bars over a period of several years. Those were the days when many ships and boats still used sail power.

Visiting the Life Saving Station is a very rewarding experience. In addition to a nice gift shop, a tour through the Life Saving Station is available. The tour guide is very knowledgeable and touring the station is a very educational experience. The station is set up exactly like it was when in use. An interesting note about the Life Saving Stations along the Atlantic Seaboard is that the stations became part of what we now know as the Coast Guard.

Chapter 15

The Oysterman

At one time, years ago, oysters were the main source of income from Delaware Bay. In the late nineteen fifties all that changed. A disease killed about eighty percent of the oysters in Delaware Bay. It started on the New Jersey side of the Bay and left the Delaware side of the Bay untouched until the following year. Oyster harvesters from New Jersey thought that the Delaware oysters were immune from the disease and purchased seed oysters from Delaware to restore their oyster beds.

Planting oysters in Delaware Bay was started in the latter half of the 1800s by a former seaman named Montgomery. He built the third or fourth house in Little Creek, Delaware. Most people have never heard his name, but at one time in the early 1900s his was a well-known name around Delaware Bay. He was considered the father of seeding oysters in the Bay. Now days, if you asked an oysterman if he has ever heard of Captain Montgomery, that man would give you a blank look and then admit that they had never heard the name.

Captain Willis Hand at the controls of his boat

The *Namu* with cargo of oysters

Capt. Hand's boat *Namu* being prepared for another season working on Delaware Bay

A good day's catch of conch

Conch traps at Bowers Beach

Winter crabs dredged from Delaware Bay

The oyster industry reached its peak in the 1920s when about 500 schooners harvested oysters on Delaware Bay. All dredging in those days had to be done while under sail. Motors could be used to get the schooners from where they were docked to open water. Most schooners had what was known as a "yawl boat" to move the schooners out into the Bay. It must have been a magnificent sight seeing all of the hundreds of schooners under sail dredging oysters. The ban on using motors was lifted in 1949. Dredging by motor power has proven to be more efficient.

One man, Frank "Thumper" Eicherly, owns the old Maggie Myers, one of the oldest schooners working Delaware Bay. It is believed that the keel of the Maggie Myers was laid in 1897. He has rigged it with a single mast. He uses a combination of sail and motor power for dredging crabs and oysters. "Thumper" has worked on the water for many years and is well known for his dedication to earn a living from the Bay and is considered an outstanding boat captain.

Once before the crab industry became the main means to earn money from the Bay there is no doubt oysters were the primary source of revenue. The wire crab pot was new to this area. Supposedly, Smith Hand purchased some of the first wire crab pots from a supply house from a village on the Chesapeake Bay. He wasn't the first to actually use them on the Bay. Several other people claim to have been first. It could have been "Dickie" Short or "Shorty" Short.

Regardless of who used those traps first, that trap changed the way crabs could be caught. Before, like some still do in the Chesapeake Bay, trot lining was used. Trot liners never did well in Delaware Bay because of the roughness and the swift tide of the Bay. The wire cages furnished the means for crabs to take the place of the once mighty oyster industry. The oystermen who wanted to still work on the water turned to crabbing. Some, like in all businesses have been successful and stuck with harvesting crabs during good and bad years.

In the mid 1950s, a young man, Willis Hand, had an aspiration to make it big in the oyster business. Willis was the son of Smith (Whiffy) Hand who owned the Hand oyster business at Port Mahon, Delaware. Some seasons Captain Hand would hire 50-150 oyster processors to work in his shucking house. Mr. Hand ran a very successful business. He had worked on the water for years and had gained vast experience raising oysters and processing them for shipment. Raising oysters meant establishing beds of shells and placing seed oysters on these artificial beds.

From his success in the oyster business, he had purchased a Packard auto dealership in Dover.
Captain Hand related that his dad sold new Packard cars to his employees with no money down with easy payments without interest. Anyone else wishing to purchase a Packard (relatives too) had to secure a loan and pay interest. Mr. Hand is remembered for his knowledge of harvesting oysters from the Bay and his good treatment of employees. He was a hard worker and expected as much from the people who worked for him.

Dredging oysters

Load of oysters just dredged

Willis Hand's Dock at Port Mahon, Delaware

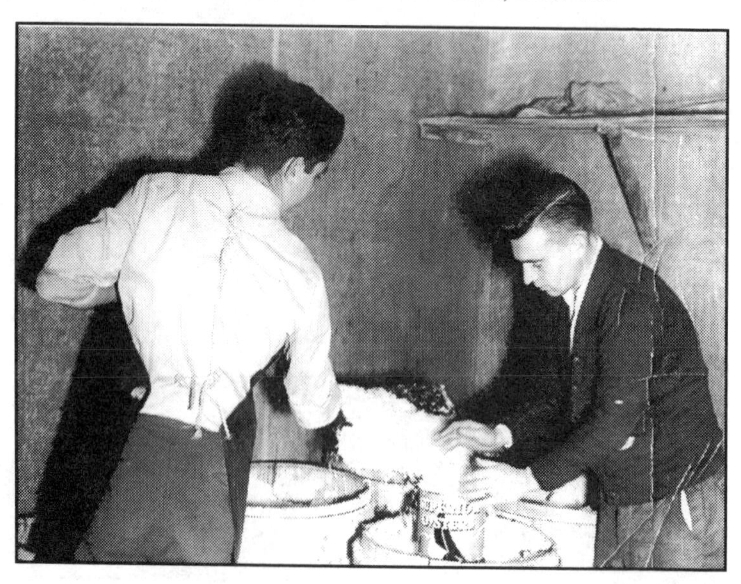

Hand's Oyster Company employees icing down cans of freshly shucked oysters in the 1940s

Unloading oysters from one of Hand's oyster boats in the early 1950s

The *Namu* and *Maggie Myers* tied up at Bowers Beach

Willis Hand worked from an early age on his father's boats and hung around the oyster processing building. As a teenager he captained an oyster boat on weekends so that the regular captain could take off. Willis' older brother, Roy, took over Smith Hand's business when he died.

Captain Roy Hand's venture lasted until he suffered a massive stroke while working on the Bay and was confined to a wheel chair for the remainder of his life. Willis then took over the oyster business. It is interesting to note that two of Roy Hand's sons followed in his footsteps and earn their livelihood from the waters of the Bay, as well as Willis' son. All are very competent and knowledgeable of working on the water. Their success on the water is the result of working with Willis Hand. He worked them hard, but treated them fairly. Working on his boat was a true learning experience.

The disaster that struck New Jersey's oyster industry also moved to the Delaware side of the Bay the following year. Willis had planted enough oysters in his leased beds that he anticipated a return of at least 8,000 bushels. To his disappointment, when he started to harvest his oysters, most brought to the surface were dead. He only caught 63 bushels of live oysters. The oyster disease that killed most of the oysters in the Delaware Bay wiped out a 4.6 million dollar industry. That was in the nineteen hundred fifties' dollars.

Captain Hand pointed out to me that raising oysters is a type of farming. The oystermen plant seed oysters in prepared shell beds and must wait three years for them to mature. Much can go wrong during that time. Just as farmers have crop failures, those who farm the water do too.

When his oysters died from the MSX disease, it was a tremendous disappointment, but he started crabbing and soon mastered the art of catching crabs. He and his son still crab in the summer and dredge crabs in the winter.

Presently, the Fish and Wildlife Scientists are working with the people who have shell fish permits to preserve and attempt to bring oysters back into the Bay. The people holding shellfish licenses are allotted a limited number of bushels of oysters to harvest each year.

Captain Willis Hand remembers his first long trip on an oyster boat. In 1943 our nation was at war. Back in those days there were few big rigs on the road like we find today. Many things were shipped by boat in the coastal areas. During a slack season, Captain Smith Hand decided to take two of his 60-foot oyster boats and travel up river to the Delaware-Chesapeake Canal and cross over into the Chesapeake Bay and down the Bay to Norfork, VA. There a canal would take them to North Carolina. He planned to pick up watermelons and take them to a market in Baltimore.

The oyster boats could carry a load of oysters or other cargo equal to their own weight. Oyster boats were real workhorses of their day. That trip was exciting and interesting to a 12 year-old. They anchored for the night near Norfolk. When they awoke the next morning they found themselves amid a practice landing by Marines. Their two boats were surrounded by Navy

Landing Craft. Being amid a Marine landing and establishing a beachhead was very exciting.

The rest of the trip was uneventful and they loaded both boats full of watermelons and took them to Baltimore Harbor. There a buyer met them and the melons were unloaded and hauled away.

Many of the oyster boats were built in the early nineteen hundreds from white oak and the boat's long life attests to the durability of white oak. Willis Hand has owned several large oyster boats and is considered the most skilled boat captain operating on the Bay. Even though he is at the age where most men would be retired or deceased, he still works with his son and nephews harvesting crabs, oysters, conch, horseshoe crabs and eel. He has served on the State Shellfish Commission and various other posts dealing with Delaware Bay. When someone needs information about working on the water or the prevailing conditions of the Bay, Captain Hand always comes in mind as a good source to contact.

Willis Hand is sometimes melancholy when he thinks of Delaware Bay and compares today's Bay with the Bay that he once knew. Just driving to his dock at Port Mahon, the road takes him past where the Hand's oyster business once operated. All that remains of a once busy enterprise is the foundation of the shucking house and posts sticking out of the water that once held living quarters for some of the many workers once employed there. Erosion and silt has destroyed his docks where years ago oyster boats tied up to off-load tons and tons of oysters.

Capt. Roy Hand's boat *L B Travis* tied up at Bowers Beach dock

The *Maggie Myers* and the *Namu* dredging for oysters

Capt. Willis Hand's boat dredging for oysters on Delaware Bay

Captain Willis Hand and a day's catch of oysters

Then as he drives around the curve on the Port Mahon road he can see other docks that he used until recently to tie up his boats and maintain his equipment. That site has also eroded and silted in. When he reaches his new docking area where his boats are presently tied up, it's like reaching the last of an era. His boats are tied to a recently repaired dock and it is like a last contest with the Bay being the winner. Because of the problem of shallow water at his dock at Port Mahon, he also works out of Bowers Beach.

At his dock at Port Mahon, he can close his eyes and the image of what the Bay once was floods through his mind. He can almost hear the laughter of busy men who worked on the water gathering together at Jenkins Wharf and in the store that was once operated at different times by Harry (Pretty) Killen, Young and Jenkins. All these men have gone to their eternal reward. Many a card game or dice gambling has taken place there. Some of the men who were young just starting on the water, would watch the older men gamble. Some large stake poker games occurred there.

One of the men didn't want his wife to know that he hung around Jenkins wharf and drank and gambled with the other men. Some times when he was winning and had a big pile of money before him, some one would yell, "Miss Ruth is coming." That man, Jack Pleasanton, would grab his winnings and run and hide so that she wouldn't catch him gambling. "Miss Ruth is coming" soon became a big joke and was used on him often. He accepted the ribbing and would later laugh at his reaction when one of the men would yell those dreaded words. Jack "Dead Eye" Pleasanton went to meet his maker in 1997. Perhaps he was eagerly waiting to hear those words again, "Miss Ruth is coming" because she went to meet him in 2006.

Captain Hand has witnessed many unusual incidents happening on the water. One day he and his wife were returning from crabbing when they sighted a small boat capsized with one man on top of the over turned boat and another man hanging onto the edge of the boat. He pulled them aboard and hoisted the small boat aboard also. One of the men had a large hook firmly imbedded in his leg. He was in considerable pain and almost passed out once he was rescued. That was an example of many that Captain Willis Hand witnessed of people being on the Bay in too small a boat. People often fail to realize how deadly the Bay can be to the unaware and unprepared boater. The Bay can be as meek as a lamb and suddenly change into a roaring lion.

Working on the Bay also had its lighter side. Capt. Hand told the story of when he and his wife were checking crab pots north of Port Mahon in very shallow water. It was low tide and his wife was driving the boat. At low tide the long ropes connecting the floats to the crab pots are stretched out on the surface and Nellie ran over two lines with the boat.

Willis became very irritated and told her, "I'd better drive the boat before you cut all our crab lines."

He took the controls and the first thing he did was to run over and smash a crab pot in the very shallow water. I imagine Nellie chuckled to herself. Willis has been blessed with a wife who supports his working on the water. In discussing material for this book, Nellie's look and enthusiasm when telling about some of the things her husband has accomplished, clearly reveals her love and adoration for him. The old quote, " Behind every successful man there is a loving wife," is evident when talking to this couple.

Captain Hand has many painful memories associated with the Bay. One that is especially painful to remember is that of the sinking of the Maine. He was an eyewitness to the Maine running aground on a bar in the Bay. The Maine had aboard Robert Steward, operator of Bob's Seafood Restaurant in Dover, Captain William Burris of Little Creek, and Michael Scott of Port Mahon. It was a foggy day and a storm suddenly came up. The Captain of the Maine knew about the bar but became confused in the fog. The Maine became hopelessly stuck on the bar.

Captain Hand saw what was happening and attempted to save the crew from the Maine that was fast being torn apart by the action of the eight to ten foot waves slamming the boat up and down on the bar. He ran aground and could have suffered the same fate as the Maine, but fortunately he was able to back his boat off the bar and raced to Port Mahon to summon help for the crew of the floundering boat. The last he saw of the three- man crew was that of them huddled on top of the boat's cabin waving for help. Irvin Jenkins, owner of Jenkins' Wharf had warned Captain Burris not to go out that day. Some people are more weather wise that others. Those men were sadly missed by all who knew them.

The Coast Guard and Base authorities were alerted and an attempt to reach and save the men was made. When help did arrive, the Maine had already broken apart and the cabin and men couldn't be found. The area was search thoroughly, but none of the men were ever found. Willis often thinks, "What could I have done different to save the crew of the Maine?" The answer is always the same, nothing.

Captain Willis Hand has experienced many dangerous situations while working on the water. Once during the winter when working the water in his sixty foot boat, the Namu, built in 1957 at a boat building business on the Chesapeake Bay, something knocked a hole in the bottom of the boat. He suspected that a metal dredge was the cause. The boat started taking on water so fast that the boat was in danger of sinking.

He radioed his son who was working on the water in another area on the Maggie S. Myers, another sixty foot dredging boat, that he was taking on water and for him to get there as fast as possible. His son, W.C. notified the Coast Guard and Jackie Donovan who owns Donovan's Docks at Bowers Beach. Donovan called the Bowers Fire Department and they brought pumps out to the Namu.

W.C. Hand rushed toward his father's position as fast as the old Maggie Myers would move. He came alongside the Namu, and being in a hurry to rescue his father and crew, slammed into the Namu and broke a rail off the side of the boat. Captain Hand attempted to move the Namu to shallow water so that if it did sink, it could be easier to salvage. Because of the bad leak and all the water in the boat he couldn't maneuver. The boat was in danger of sinking, and was going down by the stern.

Later the Coast Guard arrived with two boats and soon a helicopter lowered more pumps in an attempt to pump the water out of the Namu. The Namu was sitting low in the water with a foot and half of water in the hull. The pumps soon overcame the leak and the boat was towed to Bowers Beach and eventually repaired.

Crew members, David Williams, James Dashiell, David Williamson and Clifton Mosley, praised Captain Hand for how he calming handled a situation that could have been life threatening. They stated that they weren't worried because they had the best and most knowledgeable Captain working on Delaware Bay. Working on the water in the winter is always a tricky situation. People don't last long during the winter should they fall into the cold bay water.

Having an oyster/crabbing operation in a lonely place like Port Mahon seems to tempt thieves. Jack Pleasanton once operated a small store that sold bait, snacks, ice and fishing tackle. That shop seemed to always be targeted by thieves. The worse incident was that of someone attaching a chain or cable to the bars on the store's windows and attempting to pull the window out. Instead, they yanked the entire wall down allowing them to steal anything they might want. The Melvins who operated the store for a few years also experienced a problem with thieves. Melvin is a well-known and successful crabber who worked out of Port

Mahon for many years. While he was working on the water, his wife, Jane operated the bait shop at Mahon and kept in radio contact with her husband and other watermen. When he would come off the water after a busy morning, she would have his meal prepared and waiting for him.

Captain Hand revealed that his dock had been targeted many times by thieves. Some were nabbed, but many weren't. One day when Captain Hand and his crew arrived at his dock to work for the day they observed a young man dart under the dock in an attempt to hide. The man was ignored for a time. It was cold and the hidden man became colder all the time. He had gotten himself caught in the mud under the dock and couldn't free himself. He begged Captain Hand to free him. He was completely ignored. One of the crew called the State Police and the patrolmen dispatched had to help pull the man from the mud. I imagine that Captain Hand was so sick of people stealing from his dock that he thought it served the thief right to have to suffer in the cold mud. Maybe that man has rethought the benefits of stealing.

Captain Hand related how someone stole some of his toolboxes and a five-gallon can of gasoline. Two thieves were caught leaving the dock with a five gallon can of gasoline between them on the seat. The police came and arrested the men.

Another time someone stole the controls for his boat's radar. The controls alone weren't any good to the thief without the rest of the unit that was mounted above the cabin. Captain Hand reasoned that the thieves would return for the rest of the radar unit. Later in the night a car crept up the road toward the dock. Two men got out and walked to the boat with tools in hand to take the other part of the radar unit. They really received a surprise when Captain Hand gave them a welcome they will never forget.

Captain Hand has seen year after year pass and all the changes that have taken place on Delaware Bay with each passing year. He has hung onto working the Bay with the ferociousness of a bulldog, accepting and overcoming all the Bay has dealt him. Looking back over a lifetime working on Delaware Bay, he has few regrets about staying with his occupation. However, he doesn't encourage his grandchildren to follow in his footsteps. He sees the Bay growing more and more difficult as a place to earn a living. He's not a bragging man, but he has accomplished much during his career working on the water. When people think of those earning their living from the Bay, Captain Willis "Wilbo" Hand comes to mind. He leaves a legacy for future generations who work on the Bay to follow.

Chapter 16

The Cabin

By Paul Davis

Traveling down the Leipsic River on their way to the Delaware Bay crabbers, fishermen and local water fowl hunters must all pass a little cabin on an island directly across from the Bombay Hook Refuge. The island consists of 90 acres of marsh, and was created years ago when the Corp of Army Engineers cut through land owned by Mr. Arthur Carrow. This was done in order to make the river straighter from Leipsic to the Delaware Bay for navigational purposes. Today Arthur Carrow's son Harvey Carrow owns the farm which the island was original a part of directly adjacent to the Bombay Hook Refuge.

Before there was an island created, boats leaving Leipsic had to travel around the marshland of Arthur Carrow. It has been told on occasion on a low tide the boats had to be pulled by ropes from the back of the marsh to the Leipsic River. Mr. Arthur Carrow, known to his friends as "Bobby," was a waterfowl hunter and trapper, and at one time also had a small cabin farther down the river nearer to Delaware Bay. That land is now owned by the Bombay Hook Refuge.

In 1949 Mr. Maurice N. Jarrell, known to many on the river as " Marsh Jarrell," and William C. Holden, Sr. of Dover purchased the 90 acre island from Arthur "Bobby" Carrow with the intention of building a hunting cabin. In early 1950 preparations were made, materials purchased and construction of the cabin began. The cabin was equipped with bunk beds, a pot-bellied coal burning stove, a small kitchen containing a gas stove, gas ceiling lights, and "running water" provided by a fifty gallon rain barrel. The cabin was used year round by the families, not only for hunting in the winter, but for swimming, crabbing and picnicking in the summer. Justine Jarrell Davis remembers catching enough crabs off the dock in only a short time for the whole family, and the delicious taste as they were caught, cooked and eaten within a few hours.

After the cabin was complete, a boat dock was built, with a wooden ramp. Maurice and "Bill" with help of friends constructed their duck blinds around the island designed as a baseball field with 1st, 2nd, 3rd bases, and short stop. With the help of friends George Hynson and Joe Poyner, telephone lines were run to each blind, and each blind was equipped with a hand-cranked phone. A wall crank phone was located in the cabin known as 'home base. It connected all the phones emerged in the river, on the back of the island, leading to a crank phone at the Texas Ranch hunting club of Bill Holden, Sr. The telephone line to Texas Ranch was used for emergencies, and at the end of each day someone would call from the Texas Ranch to be sure everyone on the island was alright. As the years passed the telephone was very busy. On occasions a hunter would remain in the cabin, watch for flocks approaching, and call to give reports to various blinds. For many years friends of Maurice Jarrell and "Bill Holden" looked forward to spending time at the cabin, discussing politics, playing cards and having many good hunts. Friends joining them and spending nights at the cabin, were Delaware Governors Charles Terry and Elbert Carvel. Also visiting were friends of Governor Terry—Governor McNair of South Carolina, Dr. James McNinch, Attorney Herman C. Brown, "Eddie" Taylor, Joe Poyner, Earl Sipple, George Hynson, Leon Pleasanton, Dr. Harry Neese, Jeff Farlow and many others. It's often been said, a lot of political decisions were made while spending an evening at the "little cabin on the island."

Maurice Jarrell's son-in-law, Paul Davis of Woodside, DE recalls many conversations he had with the late Herman C. Brown while having lunch at the "Nuts" restaurant in Dover. Mr. Brown often spoke of the respect and friendship he had for Maurice Jarrell, and Bill Holden, Sr. and how he looked forward to joining them for a couple days at the cabin. Mr. Brown was known to supply steaks for the evening dinners, and some of the hunters would gather in the cabin to talk and play cards. Some of the men would prepare memorable meals. The food, drink and fellowship were legendary.

Governor Charles Terry after a successful hunt at the cabin

**George Hynson and Bill Holden, Sr.
coming from the cabin after a day of hunting**

Governor Terry at his desk
Card sent to Morris Jarrell, a good friend and hunting buddy

Around 1950-1951
Justine Jarrell Davis on the cabin's dock with hunting friends

George Hynson, Maurice Jarrell and unidentified friend showing the result of a successful day hunting ducks

Maurice Jarrell and Wilbur at duck blind on island in 1973. Wilbur was an outstanding retriever and companion for Maurice.

Governor Terry, Bill Holden, Sr. and Maurice Jarrell relaxing on the Delaware

In 1960, the National Retriever Field Trials were held at Bombay Hook Refuge. Maurice Jarrell and Bill Holden entertained the field trial judges, corporate executives and some of the dog handlers for dinner and fellowship at the cabin.

From time to time Governor Terry's boat *The Delaware* would dock at the cabin. The governor enjoyed spending time with his long time friends Maurice Jarrell and Bill Holden, Sr.

In the early days of the cabin, waterfowl hunting was at its height. Bill and Maurice kept a hunter's log to record daily hunts, containing the hunter's names, date, weather conditions, tides and amount of ducks and geese taken at each blind location. Bill Holden, Sr. was known to analyze weather conditions and tides; he could then give a fairly accurate prediction of how a day's hunt would go. According to Joe Poyner, before the end of each day Maurice would always slip into a ditch, and get wet. One day the men heard a large splash coming from the river, as Maurice had jumped in. As they pulled Maurice out of the river he said, "Well I got that over with for the day, now lets go hunting."

Maurice and Bill left Leipsic by "putting off" at the well-known dock of Jimmie Whedbee. Old timers can still imagine seeing these dedicated hunters loading their duck boats with dogs, food, guns and supplies and laughing as they headed down the river to spend time together at the cabin.

Maurice and Wilbur with Goose Wilbur just retrieved

Bill Holden, Sr., Dr. Jim McNinch, Maurice Jarrell with friends

Paul Davis with Penny getting ready for a day hunting ducks

The Cabin and Wilbur

Maurice and Wilbur setting out goose decoys

Governor Terry on the *Delaware* going to the cabin. The *Delaware* was captained by Capt. Edgar Thompson of Little Creek. He was a well known boat Captain who operated the *Delaware* for many years.

Governor Terry, Maurice Jarrell and Bill Holden, Sr. on the deck of the *Delaware* docked at the cabin

Maurice Jarrell, Bill Holden, Jr., Bill Holden, Sr. and friends with Wilbur

Maurice Jarrell returning to cabin after a good hunt

In later years when Maurice and Bill were no longer able to go to the cabin it was maintained by "Skip" Jones, who has many fine memories of his time there. Maurice and Bill are gone now, but the cabin and the marsh will remain in their families. The current owners are the sons of Bill Holden, Sr., Wayne Holden and Bill Holden, Jr. and Maurice Jarrell's grandson, Dr. Christopher Coon and Maurice's son-in-law Paul Davis, all of Dover, Delaware. Both families will always cherish the history, memories and enjoyment of the cabin. Due to the convenience of cell phones, the crank phones are no longer needed. However, the daily hunting log tradition is still used by the family, and when you look through it's pages you're reminded of the fond memories of the "little cabin on the marsh."

The history of "The Cabin" would never be complete without mention of Maurice Jarrell's constant companion on the marsh, his beloved Chesapeake Retriever "Wilbur." After a cold day of retrieving ducks and geese "Wilbur" was always given the front seat of Maurice's vehicle for the ride home to Dover. Once when a hunting buddy of Maurice's asked why they had to sit in the back and the dog, "Wilbur" enjoyed the front seat. Maurice replied, "Friend, when you jump in Leipsic River, swim through ice cold water and bring me my ducks and geese, you get the front seat by the heater." Wilbur was always allowed to enter "Sambos" Tavern in Leipsic at the end of a long day's hunt, where he would patiently sit by the door wearing his hunting cap, waiting for Maurice.

Chapter 17

Musings from the Bay

Memories of working on the water are indeed precious. In the spring, during the start of the crabbing season, I would arrive at my dock in Little Creek just as dawn was breaking. Often the tide would be high or racing out. The first thing that had to be done was unload the baskets of fish to be used for crab bait, gasoline and other equipment from the pickup.

This is a time of day when one's body works in slow motion. Maybe the mind was debating how much better it would have been to have slept in rather than preparing for a day working on Delaware Bay. When someone was with me there would be little conversation between the two of us. Matter of fact, it was easy to be a bit grumpy, so it was better to be quiet and do what had to be done in preparation to work the day on the bay.

To the East, the first light of day gave off an eerie light. Once the boat was refueled, bait was placed onboard followed by the extra five gallons of gasoline always carried to prevent being embarrassed by running out of gas or to assist other boaters that might run out of gas. In my mind there is no excuse for running out of gas. True, sometimes in rough waves the boater would use more gas than expected. I once towed a crab boat, much larger than my boat, back to Port Mahon because the crabber operating that boat had run out of gas. I used my extra can of gasoline and ran out of gas and coasted into the launching ramp at Port Mahon. The grateful crabber quickly got me another can of gas so I could make it back to Little River and my dock.

The motor would start with a cough and expel a puff of white smoke, then the motor would settle down to a gentle purring sound as it idled. Casting loose from the dock was done and the lines neatly coiled for the next time they would be required. Accelerating the boat slowly so that it would not leave a damaging wake that would cause other boats to bang against each other and the dock, I started the two- mile run to the Bay.

In the cool of the morning, with the wind in my face, I would pour on just enough power once I left my dock and moved down the river at a slow speed. Ahead of the boat, ducks would take to the air, large Grey Heron would look up in disgust at being interrupted from their fishing. Small white egrets often would ignore my passing.

Fiddler Head Crabs could be seen darting out of the mud on the shore like they sensed that the passing boat would wash them away. Ahead of the boat, in the distance, ripples in the water indicated fish feeding. Sometimes a muskrat or otter could be seen swimming across the river, and as the boat grew near, submerging.

Along the shore of the Little River one could see

tracks where deer had crossed. A boater who was observant never knew what unusual thing would happen on the scenic shores of the river. One morning, just as daylight was breaking, a large flock of birds took flight as the boat neared where they were feeding along the shore. There must have been two hundred birds in that flock. The birds were different from any the author had ever seen on the river.

Later that evening, while listening to the local news, a mention was made of a rare bird that normally lived only in Africa had been sighted at Port Mahon, Delaware. The news reporter remarked that the bird had probably been caught in a storm and blown to the North American Continent. The reporter proceeded to say that there were probably only one or two of the birds in the Port Mahon area and bird watchers should make the most of the sighting.

The boat approached the Bay and slowed for the left turn around the sand bar that once guarded the entrance to Little River and then a quick right to proceed out into the Bay. The water was flat like a tabletop, which was a rare condition. The most difficult condition for working on the Bay is when the water was choppy and the clouds hung low. The colors of most of the crab pot markers from a distance appeared black.

The white milk jugs marking the start and end of my crab line would be approached according to the direction the tide was running. The crabber should work into the incoming or outgoing tide. The first crab pot would be approached with anticipation regarding what it had caught. Often in addition to crabs, Toadfish (Oyster Crackers), small turtles and an occasional small fish could be found in the crab basket.

The crab pots had to be emptied and re-baited. Pulling the sixty-six pots by hand was a laborious task and by the time the last crab pot was pulled muscles would be aching. When the water became rough and the waves increased in size, working from a small boat sometimes resulted in becoming seasick. For those people who have never experienced seasickness, they don't know how lucky they are. When beset with sea-sickness, you start feeling so bad that you become afraid you might die. As the seasickness becomes worse, you are afraid that you won't die and be free of the agony that this condition causes.

Then, the catch had to be sorted by size and gender, the boat cleaned and then motor back to the dock. The equipment and gas tanks were loaded onto the pick-up and the crabs delivered to market. At the end of the day a crabber is a very tired individual.

Few crabbers stay up very late at night, because four AM when most crabbers start their day arrives too soon. One old fellow used to tell his sons that they could stay up as late as they wanted, but come four-thirty AM they would be expected be up and ready for work. A few of the boys who had stayed up very late and then rose early to work on the Bay had to suffer through a long tiring day. After a couple of experiences working most of the day on the Bay with only one or two hours sleep the previous night, most made it a point to get to bed early.

I can understand after having worked on the water for a few years why people attempt year after year to earn their living from Delaware Bay. Working on the water creates within a person a feeling of being in control. From not having to punch a time clock or work a straight 8-5 job under the supervision of someone else, gives a person the feeling of being their own boss. Even those men working as deck hands are yearning for the day when they can afford their own boat and work the Bay answering to no man. Working the Bay casts a spell on most people. After all these years away from working on the Bay, I still feel excited when I see the crab boats traveling back and forth checking crab pots. Even the air smells different on the water. It makes a person feel alive. So goes memories of the past.